Here in one of America's most daunting mission fields, I have coached church planters who are defeated and ready to quit, and I have assessed potential planters who have never had a major ministry setback. *Sifted* speaks to both groups. It offers profound biblical wisdom from mature mentors who understand the challenges church planters face. As one who has been deeply sifted myself in recent years, I will be giving this book away often.

— *Ross Anderson, regional church planting catalyst,*
Utah Advance Ministries

All of us face trials and challenges in life. Wayne Cordeiro's powerful book *Sifted* will equip, empower, and encourage you to experience all of God's strength in your greatest struggles.

— *Craig Groeschel, author of* Soul Detox

Sifted is a refreshing and necessary work that releases church leaders to once again chase after their first love. Peeling back the self-destructive layers of leadership with transparency and grace, *Sifted* offers as much practical application as it offers hope. It's a book every pastor, church planter, and churchgoer should read.

— *Brandon Hatmaker, author of* Barefoot Church

D0104686

sifted

OTHER BOOKS IN
THE EXPONENTIAL SERIES

EXPONENTIAL
series

Wayne Cordeiro
with FRANCIS CHAN & LARRY OSBORNE

sifted

PURSUING GROWTH THROUGH TRIALS, CHALLENGES, AND DISAPPOINTMENTS

ZONDERVAN®   Leadership❖Network·

ZONDERVAN

Sifted
Copyright © 2012 by Wayne Cordeiro

This title is also available as a Zondervan ebook. Visit www.zondervan.com/ebooks.

This title is also available in a Zondervan audio edition. Visit www.zondervan.fm.

Requests for information should be addressed to:

Zondervan, 3900 *Sparks Dr. SE, Grand Rapids, Michigan 49546*

Library of Congress Cataloging-in-Publication Data

Cordeiro, Wayne.
    Sifted : pursuing growth through trials, challenges, and disappointments /
Wayne Cordeiro with Francis Chan and Larry Osborne.
      p. cm.
    ISBN 978-0-310-49447-8 (softcover)
    1. Suffering–Religious aspects–Christianity. 2. Spiritual formation. I. Chan,
Francis, 1967– II. Osborne, Larry W., 1952– III. Title.
BV4909.C679 2012
248.8'92–dc23   2012001611

Cover design: *Plain Joe Studios*
Interior design: *Matthew Van Zomeren*

Printed in the United States of America

---

14 15 16 17 18 19 20 /DCI/ 20 19 18 17 16 15 14 13 12 11 10 9 8 7 6 5 4 3 2

Contents

Sifted: *from "to sift" (verb)*
To separate, examine closely, or question.
To pass through, sort, scrutinize, or inspect.

Introduction
The Twelfth Rep

Satan has asked to sift all of you as wheat. But I
have prayed for you ... that your faith may not fail.
And when you have turned back, strengthen your
brothers.

—*Luke 22:31–32 NIV*

A few years ago, I hired a fitness trainer to help me with my weight
training. (I don't bother with a trainer anymore; now I just let
my weight train itself.) Working with my trainer, I loaded several
plates onto the bar and positioned myself for a bench press. Pushing
the weight upward for the first ten reps was work, but I could handle
it. Then, the repetitions slowed and the arm vibrations began.

On the eleventh rep, I was convinced that I was done. The bar
seemed glued to my chest. I cried out in distress, "I'm done! Help!"

Like a gleeful schoolgirl, my trainer smiled and said, "Keep pushing! *Now* you're building muscle. *Now* it starts!"

In my mind, I was thinking, "What do you think I've been doing
for the last ten reps?" But the trainer kept up his mantra, "*Now* you're
building muscle! *Now* it begins!" He must have understood the
urgency I felt, because he reached down with two fingers and gave

me just enough assistance so I could lift the bar up, but not enough to let me rest or give up.

When I felt like I was spent, he urged me to "dig deep" for one last repetition, because that would be, in his words, the "most important rep of all."

The following morning, even though I couldn't lift my arms to shampoo my hair, I replayed that scene in my mind. I'm sure that every repetition was important, but I knew that my trainer had been right: the real development of my muscles didn't begin until I thought I was spent. On that twelfth rep, the old muscle tissue broke down, and new and hopefully greater muscle mass took its place.

Sifting is that twelfth rep. The process of sifting, coming to that moment when our strength is spent, is how God builds our faith. It's a process that forms new character, tearing away old perspectives and putting fresh truth in its place. Former habits are discarded and wrong tendencies abandoned.

It's the rep we are most tempted to skip. But it's the most important rep of all.

SIFTING AND THE TWELFTH REP

Whenever I am going through a difficult season in life or ministry, I find myself wishing that the process of sifting were optional. In Luke 22, Jesus tells his disciples that Satan has asked to sift them, as one would sift wheat on a threshing room floor to separate the good from the bad. Jesus encourages his disciples by telling them that he has prayed for them that their faith would not fail.

I don't find this very reassuring. What I'd like is for Jesus to pray that Satan would be thwarted, or even that God would dispatch angels to assist me. But that *my faith would not fail?* That doesn't sound very reassuring! Jesus, by praying this way, seems to suggest that there's a very good possibility that my faith might indeed fail. *Gulp!*

I can picture myself dangling over a cliff, yelling for help, while my friend kneels at a picnic table and tells me that he's praying that my faith will not fail. This doesn't look like the picture of friendship at all!

But here's the good news, and we'll talk more about this in the pages to come: if Jesus' prayer comes to pass—and I am confident that it will—and if my faith will stay the course, then a new caliber of confidence in God will take place that will authorize me to give strength to others.

"And when you have turned back, strengthen your brothers." When the season of sifting is finished—and the difficulties have been navigated well—we end up with a new level of faith, a quality that is not available to us by any other means. Sifting produces a clarity about who we are and what we do, giving definition to the work of ministry that produces long-term results and fruitfulness.

The real question, then, is not whether we will face failure. It is how well we will face it. How we respond to the challenges and trials in our lives and ministries makes all the difference in the world.

What do you do when things don't go as you plan?

Perhaps you've planted a church or are involved in pastoral leadership or have just undertaken a new season of ministry and things aren't going as you had hoped they would. It's easy to get caught up in an endless cycle of tweaking programs and looking for the next tool that promises to solve every problem. Eventually, frustration, discouragement, loneliness, and even anger can set in. Perhaps your marriage is off balance or your finances have you on the ropes. You find yourself continually longing and praying for breakthrough. You want so badly to get to that next step, whatever that next step looks like in your mind, but no matter how hard you try, that next step never seems to arrive.

Hold tight.

You may be in a season of sifting, and if you respond correctly, this season can be every bit as important as the time of harvest. Sifting builds the muscle of our faith, giving us the caliber of strength we will need for what lies just around the corner. Scripture tells us that the challenges we face in life happen for a reason, and the process of sifting refines us, revealing our weaknesses, exposing our self-dependence and inviting us to greater faith in God and greater dependence on his promises. Our prayer during this time is *not* that we will avoid being sifted, but that we will navigate the process well, and after we've survived, our faith will be ratified.

Let's make this personal. When the sifting begins, we all wonder, Will I survive this at all? And if I do, will I emerge on the other side strengthened, or will I fail? That's the big question. Will I have the skills, patience, and spiritual depth necessary to survive the sifting process?

A sifted person is someone who is able, by God's grace, to reflect on his experience and emerge from a time of trial with a better grasp of what matters most. He's a person who has been tested, proven capable and mature.

THE STARTING POINT OF GREAT LEADERS

If you're in a season of difficult ministry right now, you're in good company.

In the pages ahead, we provide a roadmap for successful navigation. Some of these trials we've already experienced. Some we're still facing. Know that you have guides on this journey, and as fellow travelers, we'll journey together. Take comfort in knowing that every successful leader encounters trials. For instance, consider how:

- David's training was in desert caves, hiding from his enemies, and not in the marbled halls of a palace.
- Joseph's training was in the prisons of Egypt.
- Moses was taught—and humbled—by working as a shepherd in the sands of the Sinai.
- Jacob was assigned Professor Laban as his instructor for more than fourteen years.

Each of these leaders, when faced with a difficult challenge, had the opportunity to retaliate, refuse, recant, or run. But they didn't do any of those things. Instead, they chose to push through the twelfth rep and build the real muscle of faith in the process.

The result?

- David became the greatest king Israel ever had.
- Joseph became second-in-command of all of Egypt and singlehandedly saved Israel from famine.
- Moses led two million people out of slavery.

◆ Jacob became the father of the twelve tribes and helped lay the foundation for the glorious coming of the Messiah.

God knew what he was doing.

In the chapters that follow, we'll look at three main areas of difficulty that we must navigate in ministry—heart work, home work, and hard work. Imagine each of these areas as a stormy ocean. Each holds the power to capsize us, but if we pilot the seas well, we will reach our destination. Though the crosscurrents run deep and will seek to steer us off course, the journey's end will be worth it all, if we navigate well.

—*Wayne Cordeiro*
with Francis Chan and Larry Osborne

PART ONE

heart work

Heart: *noun*
The center of total personality including will,
mind, and emotion.
 Spirit, courage, or enthusiasm. The
innermost part of a person.

Michael Plant was a pioneer, a solo ocean adventurer. The French called him the Top Gun of the seas because of his passion for sailing the wild winds. He was energized by the cross-currents of the open ocean. This may explain why he dubbed one of his circumnavigating boats the *Duracell*. But his third race around the world was different. He designed and built a $650,000 racing vessel, a lightweight fiberglass-coated, foam-core-hull sailboat that was scintillatingly fast. He named his promising winner the *Coyote*. It was equipped with the latest in technology and designed to cut through ocean currents like a sushi knife.

On October 16, 1992, Plant launched from New York and with great fanfare headed across the Atlantic toward France. The race, if he was successful, would take him over twenty-four thousand miles, and it would take nearly four months to complete. But it wasn't long into the trip before Plant began experiencing trouble. No one heard anything from him for several days. Then, on October 21, a passing Russian freighter picked up his transmission.

"I have no power," Plant told the freighter's captain, "but I'm working on the problem." He ended the transmission with his only request: "Tell Helen not to worry." Helen Davis, forty-three, was Plant's fiancée. This brief transmission was the last direct communication anyone ever had with Plant. At this juncture, Plant was almost one-third of the way across the Atlantic, some thirteen hundred miles from the spot where the *Coyote* eventually was found.

After thirty-two days, the *Coyote* was finally spotted on a Sunday morning by a Greek tanker. It was drifting upside down about 450 nautical miles north of the Azores, and there was no sign of the solo pioneer. The mast, still fully sailed, plunged some eighty-five feet into the frigid waters. The hull was intact. The keel was vertical, and it exposed the fatal problem: the eighty-four hundred pound lead keel bulb that weighted the boat had been sheared off. To this day, no one knows if it was a rogue whale, sea garbage, or just a faulty build that damaged the boat, but without the weight of the ballast, the small boat was useless against the crosscurrents and high winds of the open seas. The ballast's weight in the lowest part of the vessel would give it stability and balance in the rough seas, and without it, the vessel would become top-heavy and be easily overpowered by the angry ocean.

To put it simply, without a keel and ballast, the boat was broken.

I'm certainly not an expert on racing sailboats. I don't know all that much about marine paints, sails, and masts. But there is one crucial fact I do know: for a sailboat to navigate the open ocean, there must be more weight beneath the waterline than above it.

When God begins a season of sifting in your life, the first thing that will be tested is the ballast of your life, which is your heart. It's the weight beneath the waterline. You can't see it, but any refining of your heart will affect everything else you do. The heart is not about skill, gifting, or even calling. It's deeper still. It's the epicenter, the core of everything.

- ◆ It's where you respond to God.
- ◆ It's where you process events and deliberate decisions.
- ◆ It's the repository from which your future is shaped.
- ◆ It's that one nonnegotiable you must have intact when you launch into open waters.

The single best thing you can do during a time of sifting is to give yourself to the process and let God's work run its course. Our prayer is that this book will help you recognize and comprehend God's ways so that when you encounter the crosscurrents of a wild ocean, you'll have more weight beneath the waterline than above it, and your faith will not fail.

In the first four chapters of this book, we'll examine what happens when a leader's heart is sifted.

1

Where Sifting Begins

Can you remember where you were when you first sensed God's call to lead a church, serve in pastoral ministry, plant a church, or be a strategic member of a church planting team?

The call was likely very real, vivid, and powerful. God invited you to dream big dreams for him, and you sensed God raising you up to do a mighty work for the honor of his name. I'm betting that you could not wait to get started on this large, kingdom-oriented adventure.

Maybe your dream looked something like this:

- The church you imagined leading would be highly effective. You envisioned that God would use it in big ways to help win large numbers of people to Christ. Lives would be changed. Marriages healed. Families restored. This church would accomplish much for Jesus' kingdom.
- You had high hopes for the limitless scope of your church's influence. Following the example of Scripture, your church would be a witness to Jerusalem, Judea, and Samaria, and the ends of the earth (Acts 1:8), meaning your church would start locally in your community and then spread its influence to your city and then who knows how big it would get?
- Perhaps you imagined that your church would evolve to be unlike other churches. You intended to "do church"

differently to reach a new generation. You would meet people exactly where they were. There would be no stuffy dress code at your church. No baggage from the past. Coffee would be hot. Music would be cool. People would come to your church because they sensed a fresh moving of God's Spirit, and that pull would be irresistible. You sensed that God would move at the core of this work. The new church would gather steam, and there would be no stopping its momentum.

❧ Perhaps you dreamed of doing multiple services, or of starting different church campuses in locations throughout the city linked through video feeds. These churches would all flourish to the point where they, in turn, would start churches of their own. Maybe your dream was eventually to grow to the size where you needed to start your own church planting network. Tens of thousands of lives would be changed!

❧ The idea of helping to create a church that reaches out to the world was alluring. You desired to enter a community and be salt and light for the sake of Christ. You looked forward to sharing the gospel and being a force for justice and social action in creative and effective ways. Your vision was truly missional—to introduce Jesus to people and invite them to step closer to him.

Regardless of the specifics of your ministerial dream, it was undoubtedly noble, fueled by good intentions, and confirmed by God and other Christ-followers at several strategic places along the way. You were excited to work with the people on your team. They were your friends and colleagues, an energetic group of like-minded visionaries. Every person was committed to the call, and you were certain these people would remain your friends forever.

Your denomination was excited. Your spouse was in agreement with the call. Even your kids (if you have them) saw the vision. You all shared the same goal: to plant a church, a highly effective church. This was going to be a powerful work for the glory of God! Dream in hand, you began your ministry.

You had heart!

Now it has been a few years. How is the dream today? If you were to give an honest assessment, would you say that the work of church leadership is anything like you envisioned it?

THE LONELIEST JOB YOU'LL EVER DO

All we had when we planted our first church was heart.

We didn't have chairs, let alone a sound system. We borrowed coffee pots and sat on cafeteria tables. We used the music stands from the band room, and everyone had plenty of time to stare at the name of the school painted on the lectern. We didn't have much, but we had heart!

We were thrilled that anyone would even come to our services. Our welcoming committee formed a human gauntlet at the front door to hug attendees. By the time a newcomer was seated, he or she would have been hugged at least twelve times. Later when people described us, they said, "You'll know those New Hope people. They hug everything within ten feet."

Not only did we pour our hearts into everything we did, but we poured everything we received back into the ministry. I remember the first offering we took. We gathered $550. We were thrilled! I went to an office furniture outlet and bought chairs so we didn't have to sit on cafeteria tables anymore. The following week, the first thing my administrator did was approach the microphone and say, "We took an awesome offering of $550 last week. And you know where it is? You're sitting on it!"

I often reminded our volunteers that a mind can reach a mind, but only a heart can reach a heart. I prompted them to remember this by saying, "Don't wipe tables with a dish towel. Wipe tables with your heart." Or to the greeters, I said, "Don't pass out bulletins with your hands. Pass them out with your hearts." Several months passed, and soon we had enough money to buy our own coffee pots and even our own sound system. We bought our own music stands, and even had enough money left over to have the name of our church stamped on them. It was like a taste of heaven!

One day, after we'd been meeting for a while, a wise woman in the church pulled me aside and said, "Pastor, I see that we now have our own chairs and our own tables. We have activities and classes.

But where's the heart we used to have? I just don't sense it like I used to." And as she spoke, I sensed that she was right. We continued our activities, but over time, the amount of heart that we poured into everything diminished. We grew busy, and somewhere along the line, though we were still committed to our mission, the passion and excitement began to fade.

We lost our heart.

This happens more often than most realize, this loss of heart. Have you ever watched the reality TV show *Dirty Jobs*? The host, Mike Rowe, explores the messiest, hardest, and often strangest jobs around. Each episode shows Mike working a typical day at a different dirty job. In shows past, Rowe has worked as:

- a coal miner
- a mule logger
- a lightning rod installer
- a worm dung farmer
- a road kill cleaner
- a sewer inspector
- a hot tar roofer

I've always wondered when Mike Rowe is going to work as a minister. Church leadership is one of the toughest jobs anyone could ever do. It's emotionally, spiritually, mentally, and physically demanding. Leading a church, particularly when planting a new church or beginning a new ministry, can be a bit like starting a new business. The rumors are true: many of those who lead churches don't succeed, and the church leadership graveyard is ominously overcrowded. If you've spent time recently thinking about quitting your ministry position, rest assured you're not the first church leader to wrestle with that thought. But don't let that temptation overwhelm you, because there is hope. Others have traveled this difficult road too, and they have succeeded. Just because your ministry doesn't look like you once hoped it would, or because you feel like you don't have the heart you once did, doesn't mean that you should throw in the towel.

The reality is that most church leaders encounter great difficulty in the complicated task of planting, establishing, and guiding healthy churches. Many church leaders lose heart. Each year, four thousand new churches start across North America. Within any given five-year period, nearly twenty thousand people are working in the trenches of church planting. For a few of these planters, those first years are a dynamic, exciting time filled with one perceived success after another. But research confirms that for the majority of planters, this is typically a time of great struggle. Not only are there the logistics and dynamics of birthing a new church, but there are the struggles with loneliness and discouragement that inevitably come from working hard in an entrepreneurial, pioneering role. I was surprised to find in a recent poll that fifteen hundred ministers leave pastoral ministry every month for various reasons. That's a staggering number. For one reason or another, these leaders feel the need to end their ministry. And not only do church leaders struggle through the sifting process, many churches struggle as well. A recent poll showed that each year some thirty-five hundred congregations die in North America. That's a staggering thirty-five thousand congregations that will become extinct in the next ten years.

Regardless of the church model, ministry approach, or tradition, the bulk of church leaders face difficulties that at some point lead them to question whether they should even be in ministry in the first place. They daydream, wondering if maybe there's another line of work they could be doing, an easier one, surely. Perhaps serving as a coal miner.

Or even as a worm dung farmer.

DIAGNOSING A LOSS OF HEART

So what is it that makes church leadership, and church planting in particular, so difficult? Why do so many leaders lose heart and want to quit? The heart, metaphorically speaking, can be a tricky organ. Proverbs 4:23 gives us this warning: "Watch over your heart with all diligence, for from it flow the springs of life." There are several ways in which the pressures of ministry can lead to a loss of heart:

✦ You've planted a church, but your church has peaked at fifty people and doesn't seem to be growing any further. You're confused, disillusioned, perhaps even embarrassed. Maintaining a small, nongrowing church wasn't what you signed up for. Your dreams have died and you have become frustrated.

◆ Perhaps your church has had the opposite problem; you've grown by great leaps and bounds. You're already at three services in your first two years. But you're constantly being pulled in a dozen different directions, and frankly, you're exhausted. The never-ending stream of late nights, early mornings, and crisis interventions has left you lonely, worn out, tired, and perhaps even estranged from your friends, colleagues, spouse, and children.

◆ The church is slowly gaining speed, but the systems and policies that provide for smooth sailing aren't falling in place. It feels like you're the captain of a ship in the midst of a violent storm, but that storm never ends. Day after day, waves crash over the bow, threatening to sink your vessel with all on board.

◆ The finances simply haven't been there. You planned. You projected. You raised as much support as is appropriate. You made the sacrifices, but you're still broke. The bills always seem to outpace the giving.

◆ You planted with a team of great friends. When you first started, everyone was excited to begin the work. But you're tired now—all of you—and relationships are strained. Tasks that need to be done are falling through the cracks. There's still much work to be done, but it feels like your team (or much of your team, anyway) has run out of gas.

◆ Your church's vision was never firmly solidified to begin with. Part of your team wanted to become the next megachurch. The other part wanted to keep things simple and organic. Everyone figured the culture of your church could be worked out along the way. But now the team is divided, and it shows.

◆ Everything's going as well as can be expected, but the day-in, day-out job of being a church leader is simply overwhelming and is wearing you thin. The treadmill is always running, and you are caught in the cycle. Now the work God is doing *through* you is outpacing the amount of work he is doing *in* you.

In various places throughout this book, we're going to invite you to do some work on your own to make the content personal and to help you apply what you are learning. Right now, we invite you to take a moment to define your biggest challenge. Then, try to articulate your most consistent, heartfelt prayer for your church. Grab a pen and jot a few notes in the spaces below. How would you complete the following sentences?

◣ The biggest challenge facing me as a church leader is:

_____

_____

_____

_____

◣ God, when it comes to this church, I truly need you to:

_____

_____

_____

_____

Let me propose a radical idea. It might sound a bit strange at first. What if everything that's happening to you right now, all of the difficulties you face in your role in this church, even the pressure to lose heart, is exactly what needs to happen to you?

Yes, everything.

What if God has indeed called you to lead or plant a church, and no, you haven't misread his call? What if God is actually calling you to lead this church through a very rocky stretch of time, the current season you are now smack in the middle of, and God has a very good reason for your being in this difficult season? That's the premise of this book. Without knowing the specifics of your situation, that's what I bet is happening to you right now.

It's called being sifted.

FRUSTRATED WITH GOD
Larry Osborne

The thought process of a new church leader often goes like this: after completing his formal education, or after sensing God's call to plant a church, he automatically believes three things:

1. That he is ready to begin the work right away.
2. That he will immediately see success according to his definition of success.
3. That since God has called him to this work, he will seldom, perhaps never, encounter difficulties in the process.

So the new church leader begins the work immediately but quickly realizes he's in way over his head. Or he begins the church, but the church doesn't look anything like he envisioned. Or he encounters difficulties but wonders why God isn't making the path easier.

Those unmet expectations form the basis for disillusionment, frustration, and the longing to quit. Whatever he had hoped for hasn't been achieved, and at the end of the day, a church planter is frustrated with himself, his planting team, his denomination or network, his job, and maybe even with God.

Often, the prayers of frustration can't even be articulated yet. But if they were, they would sound something like, "God, why didn't you come through for this church in bigger ways?" Or, "God, why aren't you helping me out more?" Or, "God, why is this so hard?"

The logic behind these prayers seems straightforward:

a. God called you to lead a great church.
b. You were faithful to that calling.
c. But the church you planted seems less than great right now.

And you don't feel good about it. You don't know what to do.

The bottom line theme in our prayers is often that God could have — and should have — helped out more. But apparently he hasn't. So you wonder if something has gone wrong. The soul-searching keeps you awake at night. Perhaps you misread God's call. Perhaps you're not really a strong leader to begin with. Perhaps this church leadership thing will defeat you in the end. Perhaps you should step off the treadmill while you still can.

As you close your eyes and try to get some sleep, the thought of closing the doors on the church plant and heading into another line of work is very tempting. Maybe, you think, it *is* time to abandon ship.

Hold on. Hope is close at hand.

THE SIFTING PRINCIPLE

The concept of being sifted is seldom, perhaps never, taught in today's church leadership manuals. The majority of church leadership books out there today are about models and approaches. They are "doing" books. They will tell you how to clarify your vision or build a better team or attract more people to your church, and the like. Those books are not wrong, and Larry, Francis, and I encourage you to read and study as many of them as you can. This book, by contrast, is about being. It revolves around the personal care and leadership health of emerging leaders. It helps leaders such as you look to your core and thrive in leadership as a whole person: spiritually, physically, and emotionally.

Let me make one thing clear: I hate being sifted.

Now that I've gotten that off my chest and you realize that I'm not all that spiritual, we can get on with how to stomach this distasteful medicine. I know, I know, I'm supposed to be thankful in all things (1 Thess. 5:16), but when the struggles linger, I weaken.

It's not always the depth of the pain. It is the length of it.

As I have mentioned, a crisis is a terrible thing to waste. I guess I have become humbler, wiser, softer, more understanding through the sifting process, but forgive me, it's still distasteful. But you cannot progress without it.

The concept of being sifted has both a negative and a positive connotation. At its core, being sifted means going through challenges and trials as a leader. That's the negative. No one likes to go through trials. Yet the process is unavoidable. A leader will be sifted; that's not the question. The question is will he emerge from the sifting as a successful leader? How will he respond to the trials and challenges he faces?

Consider the following passages that describe the process of being sifted.

> Simon, Simon, Satan has asked to sift all of you as wheat. But I have prayed for you, Simon, that your faith may not fail. And when you have turned back, strengthen your brothers.
> —*Luke 22:31–32 NIV*

We often assume that whenever God opens a door for us, everything will go smoothly. But open doors always come with adversaries. In this passage, we learn that the Devil has asked for permission to sift God's disciples. In other words, many of the difficulties we face have been purposely placed in our path. As the book of Job reminds us, God, for reasons unknown to us, sometimes allows this to happen. Yet the fact that we will inevitably face challenges as a disciple of Christ and a leader in his church shouldn't leave us hopeless. Nor should we assume that challenges indicate a closed door or imply that we have failed in our calling. Jesus shows us that the sifting process has an end. When the season of sifting is behind us, we will be stronger, and with that strength we can then turn and strengthen others.

Scripturally, we know that difficulties can sometimes come to us from the Devil, yet sometimes they come directly from the hand of God. In fact, God tested all the great patriarchs of the Old Testament at one time or another, allowing them to experience difficult circumstances to try their faith, leading them to greater reliance on him. When something challenging is happening to us, we shouldn't spend too much time trying to figure out who is causing it. The choice we face is simple: will we trust God and look to him throughout the difficulty we face, regardless of the cause, or not?

I have told you these things, so that in me you may have peace. In this world you will have trouble. But take heart! I have overcome the world.

—*John 16:33 NIV*

In this passage, we learn that Jesus does not promise his disciples an easy road to travel. Rather, he acknowledges that somehow trouble finds its way into your daily calendar. If you're in any position of leadership, I have two words for you: expect trouble! Of course, you must outlast it; you musn't succumb. But you will have trouble.

Welcome to the ministry.

Again, however, this verse of warning also comes with a promise: Christ has overcome the world. When we live in Christ, resting in what he provides for us and promises us, our hearts are renewed. He is greater than the enemies we face in this world (1 John 4:4). His overcoming may take longer than you think, and it may come strangely packaged. You may lose things you wanted to keep, and keep things you wanted to lose, but he will overcome if you do not let your faith fail.

I'm still at the tail end of a two-year season in which the depth of my pain was attended by a feeling that I was trapped. I couldn't just resign and jump on a boat going to Tarshish. Feeling trapped in the pain of an unresolved situation is like spiritual waterboarding for me. And in the midst of it, I have said and done things I'm not proud of.

But the bottom line is, my faith cannot fail. I can feel like a failure, think I am a failure, but like Job, I must say, "Though he slay me, yet will I trust him." The disiciples proclaimed the same sentiment when Jesus spoke of his body and blood as communion. Many decided at that point that there were other churches more civilized than this one led by a rogue, self-proclaimed messiah. Yet his closest disciples said, "We're here. To whom shall we go? You alone have the words of eternal life."

The truth is that you *will* fail. You simply won't have what it takes when you begin. You may have the calling, the zeal, the energy, and the support. You might have the location, the invitation, and even the money. But when you begin you won't have what it takes to finish.

"What is that?" you might ask. What's missing is that inner core, the tensile strength of faith that is revealed only under strain. It is a quality of character that is tested not in port but in the open seas. And it is this testing that ratifies your calling, not your attendance at a church planters' boot camp or the board's seal of approval. Neither your degree nor the letters of commendation you receive speak to this need. It is something that can be acquired only through failure, learning your limits and learning to trust not in yourself but in the God who has called you.

> My prayer is not that you take them out of the world but that you protect them from the evil one.
>
> —*John 17:15 NIV*

In this passage, Jesus is praying for his disciples. His request is not that they will be taken out of the world. He doesn't pray that they be removed from the challenging situations they will face. Instead, he prays that God will protect them in the midst of those challenging situations. His prayer is that we don't go over the edge: throw in the towel and give in to an affair, or drug ourselves to escape the pain, or brashly end our marriages in order to feel a release from the responsibilities we can no longer handle.

Jesus knows that we are weak and that we will be frail at times, but he prays that our *faith* will not fail.

THE UNKNOWN

If we wish to follow Christ and become leaders in his church, the question is not whether we will be sifted. The Bible indicates that trials will come if you are pursuing effective Christian leadership. Sifting will happen. Know that it will happen. The only unknown is when.

The good news is that we are sifted for a reason; it's a process that leads to refinement. A sifted person looks back on his trials with a different perspective. He emerges from the process wiser, having been tested, knowing his capabilities and weaknesses. Ultimately, our prayer should not be that we are spared from this process but that we will learn to navigate it well, that when God is done with the sifting, our faith will thrive.

Most of the growth and refinement that comes from the sifting process begins when you accept that you are exactly where God wants you to be, at least for the time being. The key is that we learn not to fight against the sifting, not to fight against what God is doing in our lives, and learn to acknowledge that he is ultimately in control of the process. Practically, one of the best ways to understand and cooperate with the process is to ask yourself hard questions, questions that reveal your motives, questions that uncover the desires of your heart:

- Am I willing to lead a congregation of fifty people and do it with a sense of privilege and honor rather than with a sense of defeat?
- Can I be okay with continuing to serve in a bivocational role?
- Am I willing to serve and lead, even if I am not known or acknowledged for what I do, even if other leaders see me as a failure?
- Am I ready to allow this fledgling church to be imperfect, to rely on scramble-management and trust God in the details, letting go of control for a season?
- Am I willing to let my expectations and ambitions go unmet for a while?

These questions help us to understand the motives and desires that drive our ambition and our sense of calling. Failure, discouragement, disappointment, and difficulty often will reveal areas in our hearts where we are listening to ourselves and not to God. That's why it's important to spend time listening in the midst of this season. If we fail to listen to what God is trying to teach us through these experiences, we end up misreading God's language. Many do, and they call it quits prematurely, leaving behind a string of failed ministry attempts or church plants.

WHO WE ARE

When I started working on this book, I called upon two dear friends, Larry Osborne and Francis Chan, and we met for conversation at an office I keep in Oregon. As we talked and shared stories, each of us realized that though our experiences were quite different, we had learned some common lessons along the way. Unless otherwise noted, I (Wayne) will be using the first person voice throughout this book to keep our stories and tone consistent, but know that all of the lessons in this book come from our common conversation. We all have lived through these ideas and affirm the lessons shared.

The process of being sifted is different for each of us, yet it's always characterized by a challenging season that lasts for an extended period of time. Despite our best efforts and intentions, we have all experienced setbacks, failures, and disillusionment as leaders in the church.

LEAVING BEHIND SUCCESS (FRANCIS CHAN)

Francis and his wife planted their first church, Cornerstone, in 1994 with only thirty people. Within two months, the church grew to more than one hundred people. After six years, the church had sixteen hundred members. And then just two years later, the church exploded to a congregation of four thousand members. There was much fruit during this time, yet this was also a time of refinement and shaping by God. Though most people see the outer success — the large numbers and Francis's growing platform as a writer and speaker — most of that came after the twelfth rep, the time of sifting.

Francis's mother died while giving birth, and his stepmother died when he was nine years old. His father died when he was only twelve. These losses had a profound impact on Francis, and he grew up with a deep sense of insecurity, a feeling that there might not be a tomorrow. A few years back, Francis wrote a book called *Crazy Love*. It was a simple book that talked about how the God of the universe loves us with a radical, unconditional, and self-sacrificing love. The book immediately shot onto the *New York Times* bestseller list and ended up selling more than two million copies. The success of the church Francis planted and the widespread success of his first book were both unexpected, and these successes caused an unexpected amount of soul searching, even disillusionment, for him.

A few years before writing *Crazy Love*, Francis had taken a trip to Uganda, a trip that altered his thinking and living. This trip, and several that followed, led him to a place of deep concern for the world's poor and marginalized as he dared to ask the question, What does it look like to love my neighbor as myself? Francis and his family downsized, moving into a smaller home. He led his church in several large initiatives to collect money to give to the poor. After his book became wildly successful, Francis decided to donate the royalties to the Isaiah 58 Fund, a nonprofit organization that helps the poor internationally.

Then, in 2010, Francis surprised everyone by announcing to his congregation that he felt called to resign from his position at Cornerstone Church in Simi Valley. The blogosphere went wild. Some people wondered if he had fallen into sin and needed to resign, which wasn't the case. Others championed him and called him a hero, which also made him uncomfortable. As of this writing, Francis isn't yet sure how his new calling will take shape, but he lives each day with confidence that God is good and that God will lead him. Despite his earlier successes — a popular book and a growing church — God has Francis in a new season of life, a season of sifting. Francis's response is a great example of how to respond when this season occurs. Regardless of what we do, we live each day in the confidence that God loves us, that we belong to him, and that he is faithful to lead and guide us to become the person he wants us to be. What we do will naturally flow from who we become as the person God is shaping us into.

MORE THAN A BUILDING (LARRY OSBORNE)

Larry Osborne, the second contributor to this book, is the senior pastor at North Coast Church in Vista, California, and the author of several bestselling books, including *Sticky Church*, *Sticky Teams*, and *Ten Dumb Things Smart Christians Believe*.

In 1980, a new church plant that was meeting in the cafeteria of a high school called Larry to be their senior pastor. He was just twenty-eight years old and had no previous experience as a senior pastor. On his first Sunday, 127 adults and children gathered for worship. In the weeks, months, and years that followed, attendance declined from that original number. These tough years were a time of testing, a season of sifting (*Larry:* I refer to them as the "dark years"), and looking back Larry is aware that God was doing something vital during that time. Unknown to those involved, God was slowly putting together a solid core team of staff and elders, the team that eventually led North Coast Church into the thriving ministry it is today.

One of the key turning points in those early years was a decision they made to build the ministry of the church around small groups, which quickly became the hub of all activity and spiritual growth. After some bumps and bruises, the plan began to produce fruit, and by 1990, North Coast Church had grown to nearly eight hundred people. The church met in a rented building, and just as they were getting comfortable and seeing some growth in numbers, they lost their lease. With just enough money in the bank to buy a used car, Larry's congregation faced a tough decision: should they stretch and spend nearly two million dollars to buy and fix up a building, or should they play it safe and rent a much smaller storefront that they could easily pay for? The storefront would comfortably accommodate the current congregation but would effectively shut the door on future growth.

The leaders chose to stretch and sacrifice to buy a larger property, and their risk paid off. By 1998, more than three thousand people were attending each weekend, jam-packed into a facility with a five-hundred-seat sanctuary. It was a wild ride, and they often ran out of space. They lacked the funds and time to build a bigger facility, and so the church decided to innovate and provide an additional service using live worship and a video feed of the weekend message. Much to everyone's surprise, the gamble paid off. Their creative new approach kick-started a national movement of churches offering worship through video venues, one of the key factors leading to the growth of the multisite church movement several years later.

In 2000, the church began the process of acquiring a forty-acre property with plans to create a new campus. The plan took ten years to reach fruition, and in June 2010, the church finally moved to its new location. Today, using a combination of live worship services and video worship venues, the church meets on three campuses and offers numerous worship options every weekend with more than nine thousand people in attendance.

Larry admits that one of the biggest challenges along the way has been making sure that North Coast Church is more than a building. Though North Coast Church has won national acclaim and has been recognized as one of the ten most influential and innovative churches in America, the focus has always been on bringing the Word of God to people and letting Christ change their lives. The church does extensive community outreach, averaging nearly two service projects a day each year. Several years back, they closed the church for a weekend and held the largest weekend of service ever recorded by a single church. During a forty-eight-hour span, more than six thousand members from North Coast Church fanned across the community to complete nearly one hundred service projects. Today, they hold similar events roughly every eighteen months.

THE UNWELCOME WAGON (WAYNE CORDEIRO)

And me?

My wife, Anna, and I moved to Hilo, Hawaii, in 1984. I was thirty-one years old, and the church I began to pastor had twenty-two people. Eleven years later, the congregation had grown to nearly two thousand people. We built a new building, and everything seemed to be going well, despite the regular and intense pressures of pastoral ministry.

Then in 1995, I felt very strongly that God wanted me to start all over again—from scratch. This was a different sort of sifting process for me, a real journey of faith. I was now forty-two years old, and I sensed God asking me to plant another church 250 miles north of our current location. We had already birthed nine churches in our eleven years, and when I first sensed the call, I assumed that I'd just train up another planter and send him. But God had something else in mind. I ended up handing the leadership baton off to my assistant, and my wife and three children and I left our comfortable home and church family to start over on this new church planting adventure in Honolulu. When I arrived, I pinned a map of Honolulu on my wall. It was a city of one million people. In my mind, I would walk the streets and pray for the salvation of those living along the roads.

Sometimes I would run my hand down the streets, and I felt like I could actually sense the pain of those who resided there.

On September 10, 1995, we held our first service at the new church. The plant started off with a shout, and we quickly went off the charts. Within six months, we were averaging fifteen hundred in attendance. We were doing three services when God challenged me to do four, and then five. I was tired and spent, but the church was growing and I had no choice but to push through the twelfth rep on the bench press.

That's when the sifting began again.

A group of disgruntled pastors asked for a lunch meeting with me. I had received letters from several of them in the past months because some of their congregants had left their churches and were now attending ours. "Sheep stealer," "Watered down gospel preacher," and "It's all built on your personality" were phrases oft quoted. They even began calling our church Wayne's World. It was humorous at first, but then it started cutting deep.

In anticipation of the tribunal, I wrestled with how to respond to their allegations. I gathered my defense and rehearsed my rationale. The evening before, I wrote down my arguments and justified my actions on a sheet of paper on my nightstand. Satisfied with my line of reasoning, I crawled into bed. But I couldn't sleep. God prompted me to get on my knees again. I was secretly waiting for him to reveal an even better defense for my vindication and had my pen poised for fresh ammunition when I heard the Lord say to me, "Tomorrow you will die." That wasn't exactly what I had in mind! Again, he repeated those words: "Tomorrow you will die." Confused, I pressed him for clarity and heard him say to me, "The reason why there is so much antagonism among the leadership of this community is that no one is willing to die. I am asking that you not use any defense. Be silent, receive what they say, and die instead. There will be no victory until someone willingly chooses to die instead of win."

I have to confess that as spiritual as this all sounds, at the time I was unwilling to go there. I wrestled with God, struggling with my need to defend myself, until I was finally at peace with his request. Focusing my attention on the cross, I was reminded that Jesus didn't overcome the power of evil and sin by unleashing a legion of angels in righteous judgment. He was victorious through his willingness to suffer humiliation and die.

The following day, I chose to die. I decided that I wouldn't fight back; I wouldn't try to defend myself. At first, it felt like having my teeth drilled without nerve blockers, but I eventually saw that this was a spiritual battle, not a relational one. What was happening had more to do with what God was accomplishing for his eternal purposes than what I wanted done in the immediate, temporal future. As I listened to the stories these pastors and church leaders shared with me, I began to really understand their plight and appreciate their pain. I've heard someone say that faith can be defined as living in advance what you will understand only in reverse. Approaching this event, I know that I was clueless, knowing only what God had revealed to me. There were no guarantees. All I had was faith.

Today, I enjoy good relationships with the pastors in our area. Most of the tensions and bitter resentment have been resolved. Our church averages fourteen thousand people and nine satellite campuses, and more than 110,000 people have made first-time decisions to become Christians. We've also planted twenty other New Hope churches on Oahu, and 122 churches throughout the Pacific Rim and beyond, including campuses in Hawaii, Las Vegas, Seattle, Los Angeles, Montana, the Philippines, Japan, Myanmar, and Australia.

But the sifting process is never truly over, even though there are seasons of greater trial. The Lord has recently been taking me through yet another season. In 2008, the blistering pace of my ministry patterns and work habits caught up with me, and I found myself flat on my back in a hospital in California undergoing emergency heart surgery. By God's grace, I survived, but I knew I needed to change the way I lived. I had been going too fast for too long, and God had a new message for me — that church leadership is as much about being as it is about doing, one of the core messages of this book.

WHEN YOU'RE BEING SIFTED

And you?

The specifics of your story are undoubtedly different from ours. Yet among you and me and Larry and Francis, we all share many common traits and goals. We all want to see the gospel advanced. We all want to see healthy churches established throughout the world. We all, ultimately, want to follow Jesus Christ with all our hearts. And we've all felt the Lord saying "no" or "wait" to us in seasons when we've wanted him to say "yes."

The bottom line, what we're all hoping for in the end is thriving church leaders of great and godly character establishing new congregations for the glory of God. We want you to be involved in significant, effective ministry, and at the same time to learn how to maintain your heart through the difficult stretches.

Our encouragement is that, rather than fighting this season of sifting, you learn the language of God, that you cooperate with what he is doing. Keep pressing the weight you are holding even though you may feel like quitting. God has promised to give you just enough assistance to lift the weight while still building the necessary depth of character and strength that he intends to develop in you. God will do something *through* you when you first allow him to do something *in* you.

REMEMBER

God must first accomplish something *in* you before he can accomplish something *through* you.

2

Identifying the Two Greatest Days of Your Life

I'd like to start this chapter by raising a question that, for better or worse, many church leaders ask about themselves or their colleagues. It's an honest question we all think about from time to time. Picture two pastors, both thirty-four years old. They attended the same university, the same seminary, and they earned the same degrees. Both are skilled, gifted men, committed to the gospel of Jesus Christ, but their callings in ministry are radically different.

So which of these two leaders is more successful?

To answer that question, we would naturally want to know what they have done. How effective have they been in their ministry?

The first man planted a church in an upscale suburb of an affluent American city. The people who come to his church are mostly high achievers with young families. The planter is dynamic, personable, and a strong communicator. He preaches directly from God's Word, and his church has exploded in growth.

Ten years into his ministry, his church is now running five services and can count several thousand first time decisions for Christ, as well as thousands of other lives touched for the sake of the gospel. By all outward appearances, this planter has done exactly what God has asked of him.

The other man moved to another large American city and began an outreach-oriented church that ministers to an ethnic subset of people. This group of people has traditionally been closed to the gospel. In fact, those who convert to Christianity within this subculture are often ridiculed by their families and friends. Sometimes relational ties are cut off altogether. This minister cannot overtly advertise or even talk about his church for fear of reprisal from leaders in the ethnic community he is trying to reach.

Ten years into his ministry, the church that meets in his house numbers eight people. In the time since he began the work, he has had many spiritual conversations with people about the person and ministry of Jesus Christ, but he has seen very few conversions.

Let's think about that question again: Which leader is more successful?

Are you wrestling with the answer to that right now?

You see, theologically we can reason out this question and agree that both leaders are being faithful to their calling, that God measures success by faithfulness and not by numbers. We might say that in God's eyes, both of these leaders are equally successful. And I believe that's right. Both of these leaders have been faithful to the work God has called them to do.

But here is the harder question, the question that reveals our heart.

Which one would you rather be?

THE URGE TO COMPARE

We live in an age when it's easier than ever to compare ourselves with others. Statistics and numbers are everywhere, and we can easily compare our church with others on the basis of number of attendees, baptisms, or some other metric for measuring growth and success. In an instant, we can see the number of our Facebook fans, the number of Twitter followers hanging on our every thought, the number of hits on our blog, the number of times a sermon has been viewed, and just about any other number you could possibly want to know.

We can also visit the website for another church and see exactly what that church is doing. We can find out information about their size, accolades, reach, scope, and influence. We can look at the personal webpage or Wikipedia page for any other pastor and can see the articles and books that other pastors are writing. We can see their daily and monthly speaking schedules. We have instant access to how big they—and we—are (or aren't). And all of this creates an enormous temptation for church leaders, the temptation of comparison. We can tell ourselves that what matters is faithfulness, doing what God has called us to do. But the temptation to compare often lies dormant in our hearts, emerging anytime we ask ourselves, How am I stacking up against everybody else?

Studies have consistently demonstrated that one of the most challenging personal issues for those planting churches, and for any church leader, for that matter, is self-worth. Leaders face temptation in this area every time we look at another ministry and wonder why ours isn't seeing the same level of success. Or perhaps we look at another church's number of services, congregation size, or number of converts in a given year and find assurance and a sense of achievement in the knowledge that we are doing better. We look at what others do and tell ourselves that we deliberately won't model our churches after something we've seen, or we do the opposite and copy what we admire or appreciate. We compare ourselves with another leader and either feel competitive, like we can do better, or inadequate, like we'll never measure up. We fall into one of the most common traps of church leadership: we stop incarnating and start imitating.

Here are some questions to consider:

* When you hear about another ministry leader experiencing numerical success, what immediately goes through your mind? Are you happy for him? Or do you feel frustrated that those numbers aren't reflected at your church? Does hearing about another church's numbers prompt a sense of competition, or even jealousy?
* Have you ever looked at the success of another pastor or church plant and whispered to yourself, "Why couldn't that be me?"
* If another church in your town is doing a specific type of

ministry, have you ever felt the need to duplicate the ministry or match its size? For instance, "They've planned four Christmas Eve services, so we should do the same."

* Have you ever felt envious of "the deal" another pastor has received, whether in salary, support, building availability, speaking events, book contracts, or number of people in attendance at his church?

* When you've checked out the website of another church or pastor and it looks like the church or ministry is taking off, how do you genuinely feel in that moment? Are you pleased that ministry is advancing? Or do you feel jealous, frustrated, or inadequate?

* Have you ever visited a church with spectacular programming and dismissed it by saying something like, "Well, the gospel isn't entertainment like they are presenting. The church is not Las Vegas! It's the bride of Christ," when what you're really feeling is insecure or inferior to what you've just seen?

Many pastors ask me about my thoughts on the emerging missional church or ask what I think about house churches. I simply tell them that I am glad for them all. "But," they reply, "these guys categorize you and other megachurch pastors as spiritually diluted and only 'crowd oriented.'"

"Ever see a competitive freestyle swimmer?" I ask. Swimmers spring off from one end of the pool, and when they get to the other end, they curl under the water and catapult their bodies in the opposite direction by pushing off the wall. This gives them propulsion and thrust. We do that with other ministries or leaders that we may not understand. We push off of the megachurch by emphasizing something we disagree with, and it gives us power and drive for our perspective. We push off of a style or we shove against something to get propulsion from it. Don't do that. Everyone needs to be able to stand on their own without comparing what they do with what others do. You can't gain lasting momentum by building your vision in response to another person's ministry.

Take a moment right now to ask yourself some hard questions. Grab a pencil and jot down your response on the following page. How would you answer the following prompt?

◆ When I'm tempted to compare myself (or my ministry)
with another leader (or ministry), the temptation often
looks like this:

_____

_____

_____

_____

This question of comparison really boils down to what we believe
about success. Does our idea of success relate to faithfulness, or is our
notion of success more about influence? Or is it about something else
entirely? The answer is found in the Word of God. How does God
determine our success? And how do we learn to serve him in a way
that avoids the trap of constant comparison with others?

IF ALL OF THE BODY WERE AN EYE

In many areas of life, success follows a progressive and linear pathway. Winning a race, for instance, is all about who gets to the finish
line the fastest. When taking a test in school, success is determined
by getting a grade, the higher the better, preferably. In this paradigm, success is defined by superlatives—a person is most successful when he is first, quickest, biggest, best, greatest, richest, smartest,
and so on.

But success in ministry is defined by a paradoxical paradigm.
Jesus said, "Anyone who wants to be first must be the very last,
and the servant of all" (Mark 9:35 NIV). Or consider the hall of
fame in Hebrews 11. The people listed there "did not receive the
things promised" (Heb. 11:13 NIV). Though they are acclaimed as
examples of faith, if one were to judge based on outward appearance
alone, they would all be considered failures. If we want to understand what it means to be successful as a church leader, we must start
by throwing out our cultural paradigms and learning to embrace
what the Bible says.

Understood this way, success as a church leader does *not* come from being:

- first
- quickest
- biggest
- best
- greatest
- richest
- smartest

What does it mean, then, to be successful as a church leader?

The Bible points us to an unlikely image to help us define success: a body. The theme of 1 Corinthians 12 is familiar territory to most church leaders. We all know that Paul talks about how the church is united, like a person's body is united, yet still composed of many parts. God gives different gifts to different people for the common good. One is given the message of wisdom through the Spirit, another the message of knowledge, another faith, another gifts of healing, another interpretation of tongues, and so on.

In the past, Christians have measured success by focusing on *unity*. That's a good start, but how do we define unity? What makes an anatomical body function with seamless unity? How does a body get all of its parts, so different and unique, to function as a united whole with perfect coordination? Thinking about the body helps us to see that unity is not having all the parts doing exactly the same thing. The stomach cannot expect the liver to function just like the stomach does. That kind of unity for a body spells "D-E-A-D."

A better definition of unity in the body is when the stomach acts like a stomach and the liver functions like a liver. True success does not come from different organs comparing themselves with one another, striving to see which is best or most useful. Instead, it comes as they support and applaud the important and distinctive role each plays, even though the heart may be constantly tempted to focus on just how temporal the fingernail is. A body functions best when each of its parts supports the differing functions of each member. Different gifts are given by the same Spirit, and they're all for the common good. How strange would it be, Paul quips, if a foot said, "Because

I am not a hand, I do not belong to the body" (1 Cor. 12:15 NIV)? Or if an ear compared itself with an eye and wondered why it doesn't perform the same function? Or if a body was just one gigantic nose, what else could be accomplished other than smelling?

The point Paul makes is that the Christian community is designed to function as a team. People within that team have different functions, and that's expected, even necessary. Comparisons don't work in this paradigm because the set up pits apples against oranges, or mini-cycles against Mack trucks. The goal is not equality or similarity, it's a mature embrace of diversity, a recognition that the team moves forward only when functioning as a whole, with each member contributing to the big-picture success.

As the Bible defines it, your success as a church leader comes from being:

- aware of your specific gifting, and
- faithful in practicing your gifting for the honor of Jesus' name.

What is your specific contribution to the body of Christ? Take a moment to articulate what you know about your gifting. Grab a pencil and jot down your response in the spaces below.

◆ My greatest strengths in ministry are:

_____

_____

_____

_____

◆ My greatest areas of weakness in ministry are:

_____

_____

_____

_____

SAME TEAM, DIFFERENT POSITIONS
Larry Osborne

Picture it this way. On any baseball team you find nine positions — the shortstop, catcher, pitcher, right fielder, and so on. But what would happen if each player wanted to be the pitcher? You'd have nine players all crammed on the mound, each elbowing for room to wind up for a pitch, everyone frustrated as nine balls are hurled toward one batter. If a team is made up of all pitchers, who's going to catch? And who's going to be an outfielder? It just doesn't work.

The same line of reasoning applies anytime we're tempted to compare ourselves with others. Some church leaders are called to be pitchers. Others are called to be catchers. Some are coaches, and some play left field. The better we understand our gifting, the better we are equipped to play our position to the glory of God.

Are you practicing your gifts to the full extent you're able, not looking down at leaders with different gifting, and not wishing you had gifts that other leaders have? Those are the first questions to ask when defining success as a church leader.

THE TWO GREATEST DAYS IN YOUR LIFE

I tell people that the two greatest days in your life are the day you were born and the day you discovered what you were born for. That's not necessarily your job. Your job is simply what you get paid for. Your calling is what you were made for. Your calling is the unique way God has invited you to express your love for him and to demonstrate his love for you as his beloved son or daughter. It's being and doing what God made you to be and to do. Discovering and accepting your calling is an important marker of a leader's surrender to God and one of the keys to battling the temptation to compare yourself with others.

Often, we compare ourselves with others because we aren't secure in our identity. We aren't sure who we really are. To avoid comparing yourself with others, ask yourself two questions: What did God truly call you to do, and who does he truly call you to be? You may not know exactly what you are called to do, but you can have a pretty clear idea of who you are, your core identity. On this basis you can focus on what you are being specifically asked to do and with wholehearted commitment begin to do only that. If you're not exactly there yet, you can begin taking steps in that direction. When you are sure of your calling, you are less prone to compare yourself with others, because you know that they are called to do something uniquely different. You are called to be you. You are not called to be someone else.

So how does a church leader go about discovering his skill set, gifting, and call?

I like to start out by thinking of it this way. What if you had all the money and resources you needed? Let's assume that you inherited five million dollars, so you had no need to work another day. Your bills were paid and you were officially retired. Now, if you are anything like me, I can't just sit around with a fishing line in a pond waiting for a bored perch or bluegill to brighten my day. So, what would I do even though I was retired?

This is fresh in my mind because I recently went through this exercise with a few counselors and coaches. I shared with them that if I retired today, I would still:

1. Preach the gospel and lead people to Christ
2. Write books and develop relevant resources
3. Train emerging leaders to plant churches

Even if I had no need to work, I would still want to do those things. If that is true, then why not do those things now? If I could delimit my life to those basic indispensables, I could probably keep going until Jesus returns! So that's what I'm doing.

If earning money wasn't an object to how you spend your day, what would *you* do?

Another way to determine skill set, gifting, and call, particularly if you are just beginning the process, involves something called "hindsight revelation." Larry Osborne regularly encourages others not to spend too much time trying to figure out the exact nature of their calling. Instead, we need to remember that God's will can often be recognized best in past tense. The initial call often is simply to start moving as best as you can, with all the passion, energy, and drive God gives you, in a direction that seems right at the time, in a direction you believe God is leading you. In other words, just do *something*. Start. Begin the good work. If you never begin, you will never accomplish anything. And that's where many people get stuck. They spend years trying to figure out exactly what God is calling them to do, and they end up doing nothing of substance or purpose. When you begin to act, following the Lord each day in obedience even when you don't have a full grasp of your calling, you'll find that along the way God will confirm whether the direction you are taking is where he wants you to head. Often, in hindsight, you will be able to say, "This was God's will for my life."

A lot of us are on a frenzied search to discover God's will before we stick out a toe, and we have a romanticized idea that if we're walking with God in the right way, we will always know his calling ahead of time. True, the promise all the way through Scripture is that God will lead his people, but the promise does not necessarily guarantee clarity, and there is an important but subtle distinction to be made between the two: the certainty that he will lead and the clarity of the leading. First Corinthians 16:5 – 7 (NIV) gives us a key insight into this distinction as seen in Paul's life: "After I go through Macedonia, I will come to you — for I will be going through Macedonia. Perhaps I will stay with you for a while, or even spend the winter, so that you can help me on my journey, wherever I go. For I do not want to see you now and make only a passing visit; I hope to spend some time with you, if the Lord permits."

Two key words are found in that passage: *perhaps* and *if.*

Read it again.

"Perhaps I will stay with you for a while ... if the Lord permits."

Do you see the lack of clarity in Paul's plans? These are not the writings of a man who's been given a crystal clear blueprint for ministry ahead of time. The normative Christian experience, even when we're in the center of God's will, is that we seldom receive a clear view out the front windshield. Usually we see much more clearly out the rearview mirror.

Note one further complication to all of this. Even when your calling is secure, either ahead of you or behind you, you will still encounter difficulties. After you have journeyed through a time of sifting, you can look back and see difficulties as being part of God's allowed plan. In the next verses of that passage, 1 Corinthians 16:8–9, Paul notes how a great door for effective work has opened for him in Ephesus, but he also notes that "there are many who oppose me." In other words, an open door does not necessarily mean smooth sailing. Knowing this fact about a calling—that difficulties should be expected—helps you stay the course.

Having a sense that your calling is secure helps you endure. While pursuing the vision God has given you, you are going to want to quit many times. But you need to constantly remind yourself of what God has called you to, so you won't drift away. Again, this is part of the surrendering process at work—when we surrender to Christ and to the call he gives us, there may be other things we want to do, but our calling will continue to bring us back to the first work.

Take some time right now to articulate your specific calling. How would you answer the following questions?

◗ When I describe the specific ministry I believe God has called me to, this is what it looks like:

_____

_____

_____

_____

◗ If I were to capitalize on my greatest strengths and successes, my ministry would look like:

_____

_____

_____

MAKE YOUR CALLING SURE

Let's look even more closely at the question of calling: what does it mean to be sure of your calling? Second Peter 1:10 (NIV) exhorts believers to "make every effort to confirm your calling and election. For if you do these things, you will never stumble." Certainly, there is a salvation-oriented application to that verse—understanding who you are as a child of God, saved by Christ. But there is an additional application of making certain of your place in the body of Christ. The writer exhorts believers to make certain of their purpose in ministry. Being sure of your calling means understanding your specific gifting and then working in that area with obedience and passion.

Let's say you sense that God has called you to be a start-up pastor for a suburban church. You understand that God has given you specific skills of vision casting, courage, entrepreneurialism, marketing, and persistence. You also know enough about yourself to grasp that God has *not* given you specific skills of teaching, compassion, counseling, or management. What do you do?

The simple answer is that you examine your gifting, your passion, and your initial calling and then work in that area until he tells you differently. With your skill set, you know you are uniquely qualified to start a church. Not everybody can do this. Yet *you* can do it well; you, far better than most, can begin a church. Thus, you begin the work. You plant a church.

In this scenario, perhaps you encounter difficulties when you examine the work of church planting with a long-term perspective. You have neither desire nor gifting to lead a group of people into a deepening relationship with Christ through the ministry of speaking. Plus, you can't stand the thought of doing hospital visitation. And you are forever butting heads with the other members of your planting team. In fact, the longer you work in your church plant and the more established the church becomes, the more frustrated you become.

In this case, it may be that your calling is to start a church, to get it up and running, and then to hand over the reins to a different pastor who can minister to that body long term. Perhaps, if the Lord permits, you will be able to start another church somewhere else.

Perhaps God is telling you to be a church planter, and only a church planter. If that's the case, then thank God he has given you your unique and needed skill set.

It's also possible, however, that God isn't calling you to quit just yet; maybe he wants you to make sure the plant is firmly established before you hand it off to a pastor who can lead the church long term. Or perhaps God wants to develop within you some of the skills for a longer-term ministry. There may be a variety of reasons why God wants you to stick it out through a difficult season. Don't mistake a season of sifting as a sign that God wants you to stop. What matters is that you avoid the temptation of comparison in this time. If you begin to compare yourself with someone else's ministry, you will feel either competitive or frustrated. Being sure of your calling often means being faithful to where God has placed you in light of your gifting and looking to him for specific direction on timing—not comparing yourself with others and trying to measure up to their calling and gifting.

Consider another example. Perhaps you know the Lord has called you to a strong speaking and teaching ministry. You've planted your church and it's growing slowly, even though many days are very frustrating. Still, you are able to exercise your gifting in your church plant, and, by and large, you feel a sense of peace there, despite the difficult days. You are well connected to a number of networks, and from time to time other job offers come your way. A missions board phones you with an administrative job, for example, or an old friend from seminary emails you, looking for a Christian education pastor for his church. Both offers look tempting because they would release you from the difficulties of your current job, but deep down you know that God has called you to be where you are. So you stay. This is good, and it is what God wants for your life. You are making your own calling certain, affirming it, and with it solidly in place, you are less tempted to compare your position with other offers.

This is one of the keys to long-term ministerial success: know how God has gifted you, know where God has called you to be, and then function faithfully in that role. You don't need to compare yourself with others because you know God has gifted you differently than others and has called you to a different place than others.

Success is not defined by seeing how you stack up against others but by being aware of your specific gifting and by being faithful in practicing your gifting for the sake of Jesus' name.

THE HUMILITY FACTOR

The process of making your calling sure is not easy. It can be a messy process. Church planters often wonder:

◆ If an open door doesn't mean smooth sailing, how can a leader be sure that he's operating within his sphere of gifting and calling?

◆ If a leader is encountering many difficulties, does it mean that he is simply encountering inevitable opposition, or should he get a different line of work?

◆ What does a leader do when he's not sure how to proceed?

There are no simple answers to these questions, but one key factor is humility.

It may sound strange at first, but in any true ministerial calling there must always be a measure of humility. Not timidity. Humility and timidity are not synonymous. Humility is expressed with teachability instead of gullibility. One man defined humility as the "gentle bow of a branch laden with fruit."

Humility is also the strength to do what God has assigned you to do. It isn't necessarily what you are capable of doing. You may be capable of accomplishing much, but the question remains how much God has assigned to you in this season of your life.

Remember this: in the end, God will not hold us accountable for how much we have done. He will hold us accountable for how much of what he has asked us to do that we have done.

Ultimately, our calling is not ours to decide. After all, it is God who calls us, and he does not call us on the basis of any unique or special talents, abilities, or skills. Our calling begins with God's dream for our lives, his plans and purposes, which exist long before they are our dreams. God invited us to participate in his work with him, not the other way around. God is in charge, not you or me. We are merely along for the ride, and God will lead us in a new direction when the time is right. When you are humble, you no longer see yourself as indispensible. Too many leaders get caught up in the practical needs and demands of ministry and forget that it is God's purposes and plans that shape our calling and ensure our success. Many leaders take this upon themselves, believing that the success or failure of a church plant or the discipling of people and saving of lost souls is ultimately determined by their efforts. A humble leader realizes that the success of his dream ultimately rests on God's shoulders.

God is sovereign. Remembering that simple and yet complex truth keeps us humble. God is always ultimately in control. Soaking in the knowledge of God's sovereignty helps take the pressure off. It brings encouragement when circumstances around us seem out of control. God still asks that we pour out our hearts for him. He invites us to press forward strenuously, exerting our best efforts and working in all that we do for the sake of his glory. Imagine the good it would do for the church leadership community if we continually kept in focus the vision of God that Isaiah is given in Isaiah 6. In this chapter, Isaiah sees God high and exalted, seated on the throne, and the train of his robe fills the temple with light and glory. The angels are continually crying out, declaring his holiness. Take a moment to picture yourself in relation to God. Remember his position as Lord. Now, in light of that vision, what is he calling you to do?

The answer is not self-exaltation. The answer is not that he wants you to be a success in the way we often define it. True success for leaders in God's kingdom begins when we kneel before an almighty God. If there's anything the church needs today it's a renewed sense of reverence and awe about who it is that we're serving. On a regular basis, we need to meditate on the biblical vision of God in heaven sitting on his throne. You may even want to get on your knees, in humility, and literally bow before God's throne. Successful leaders know that it's not about them. Whenever ministry revolves around us, we skew the horizon, and whenever the horizon is skewed, the epicenter has shifted.

I want to close this chapter by asking you as a fellow leader no longer to compare yourself with others. Give God time to define and implement his dream within your life. It may be a large dream. It may be small. Just remember that every night, we go back to the servants' quarters.

Focus your attention on contribution, not just achievement. Contribution keeps us in the servant's seat, while achievement nudges us into the driver's seat. Each of us can make a contribution, and when we do, we find our achievements to be far greater than we had ever imagined.

That's where we find our greatest rest.

REMEMBER
In the end, God will not hold us accountable for the things we have done. He will hold us accountable for how much of what he asked us to do that we have done.

3

Expectations, Criticism, and Crises

A friend of mine, Alex Daniels, is a stunt man. Early on in his career he learned how to fall, which has been essential to his longevity. He visited me some time ago, and while walking down the stairs into our lobby, he decided to trip. Yes, you read that right—he *decided* to trip.

His body hurled headlong down the last few stairs with great commotion, and then he lay motionless on the tile floor. Our two unsuspecting receptionists screamed. One sat frozen; the other began dialing 911. I started hunting for our liability insurance papers. In an instant, Alex sat up and had a good laugh. Falling down the stairs was simply part of what he could do as a stunt man.

Many actors, even if they aren't stunt men, must also learn to fall. As a child, I was riveted by watching them leap from moving trains, from horses at full gallop, and from run-away stagecoaches. Even athletes learn to fall. Most people who have played sports have at some point had a coach teach them how to dive and roll. Judo enthusiasts and those who practice the martial arts all learn, as one of their primary lessons, how to fall. So do dancers and rock climbers.

For the most part, we never learn this as Christian leaders. Many of us fall poorly. When others criticize or critique the work we put so much effort into, we grow defensive or take it personally. When we fail at a service, are unsuccessful after taking a risk, or trip over our own ineptitude, we show that we are vulnerable, that we have not learned how to protect ourselves and fend off attacks. Often, the injury we receive affects not only us but our ministries. We try to meet the expectations that others have of us, which can be well-intentioned but can also feel relentless and insatiable. Many leaders fall because they feel they can no longer bear the weight of responsibility, meeting the expectations of others, living up to their standards.

Everyone in pastoral ministry and church leadership grapples with this at some point. It's the vice-like heaviness that comes from regularly dealing with expectations, criticisms, and crises — the ongoing stress and pressure of ministry.

THE LOOK

A friend of mine recently changed careers after being in pastoral ministry for nearly a decade. I asked him how his new job was going. "Really well," he said. "These days, people get mad at me only once or twice a year. But when I was in pastoral ministry, it seemed like someone was mad at me every other day."

I found it telling — and disheartening — that this man defined his years in pastoral ministry by the amount of criticism that came his way. The tragedy is that he is undoubtedly not alone in his description of pastoral life. Sometimes pressure catches up with church leaders. Surely it can emerge in burnout. But it appears in other ways, often more subtly. A friend of mine regularly attends regional pastors' networks where about a hundred leaders gather to pray, worship, and connect. He describes the consistent level of angst he sees on the faces and hears in the stories of these leaders. One might think that a room full of pastors, who are on the front lines of seeing people saved and lives changed, would be filled with joy and radiance, similar to the angels' demeanor in heaven (Luke 15:10). Instead, he says, these leaders are consistently characterized by heavy hearts, sagging shoulders, and troubled faces. They are more like soldiers coming in from the trenches, footsore, exhausted, and sad.

THE PRESSURE OF THE CALLING
Larry Osborne and Francis Chan

A colleague and friend, Scott Thomas, is president of the church planting network Acts 29. He has shared with us the dire need he sees for effective coaching of church planters on two levels: equipping planters to plant an effective church *as well as* nurturing their spiritual, physical, emotional, and mental health.

Heartbreakingly, one Texas church planter in the network took his life last year, and Scott wrestled with how the network would address the tragedy, both to minister to the family and church and to help prevent it from happening again. Tragically, that same year, a second pastor died after what was regarded initially to be an accidental drug overdose. The medical examiner later declared it a suicide, and Scott knew that the network needed to address this severe problem of church planters struggling under the pressure of their callings.

"Both of the pastors were seemingly successful in their churches," Scott said. "Both were speaking, writing, and coaching other pastors. Yet both had been deeply troubled for years. One pastor had marital struggles. The other, we later discovered, was addicted to sleeping pills. Both had friends, families, and mentors speaking into their lives, but it appears that neither leader availed himself of help from people who could address their years of chronic pain, layers of marital issues, addictions, and underlying anger and fears."

Scott told us about how he spoke to one of the widows a short time after her husband's death. "It was very sobering," Scott said. "She told me that her husband didn't just come home one day and explode. Instead, she said, 'his soul just faded out slowly.' I'm concerned for the souls of church leaders. It's a huge mistake for any network to focus only on the success of the church plant."

Acts 29 has since taken strategic steps to address the challenges not only of planting churches but of shepherding pastors and church leaders. Programs and opportunities are now in place to help planters become qualified, gospel-empowered, healthy, disciple-making followers of Jesus who are well equipped to lead others to Jesus for the long haul.

The question remains for each of us involved in church leadership: How do we handle pressure? Picture that room full of pastors again. Is that who we really are—grim-faced leaders worn out from our time in the trenches? Or can we learn to thrive within this calling, to recognize that regularly dealing with expectations, criticisms, and crises is part of the job and yet to remain undefeated by the pressure?

OVERWHELMING EXPECTATIONS

If you are in a season of sifting that is predominately characterized by an excessive amount of pressure, the simple encouragement we have is to stay the course. We're not here to offer you quick fixes or easy solutions; rather, we want to emphasize the core message of this book: sifting happens, but God is still in control, and in fact God uses this season for your good because he wants to do something in you before he does something through you.

Larry, Francis, and I can all recall seasons of sifting when the pressures of ministry felt overwhelming, when we needed to minister to hurting people for long periods of time, or when we needed to perform too many funerals in too few days. There were seemingly unending seasons when people were disgruntled with the church or with us or when crises came at the most inconvenient times. A couple whose baby died from sudden infant death syndrome. A teenager killed on graduation night. A young fiancé diagnosed with a rare form of cancer. A colleague jailed for impropriety. The world can be a tragic place, and pastors are indeed on the front lines of ministering to people at their highest and lowest moments.

When I think back to my own years in pastoral ministry, I can picture the parents of a teenager crying in my office, sad that their son was walking down the wrong path, desperate for help from the church, expectant and even demanding that I intervene in their son's life. "Why doesn't this church offer a better youth group?" they screamed.

I remember an angry keyboardist, frustrated that our church's worship team was not using him, in his words, "to his full potential." He expected that he would regularly be given a predominant role in the worship service, and his expectations were not being met. "I really think the worship here should better utilize people," he said.

I can picture a man donating computer equipment to the church with the mandate that he was going to donate the equipment "only if it was going to be well used." I remember another man who gave $65,000 to the church but kept pulling on invisible strings, demanding that it be used as he directed. Three weeks later, after sleepless nights of wrestling with his demands and threats, I had our accountant write a check for $65,000, and I gave it back to the demanding donor.

These frontline stories of pastoral work are endless. To be sure, it is a demanding profession, but it is never dull! So how do we navigate through people's expectations of us and still be okay? How do we handle expectations, learn to get over them or live with them, or even learn from them? There are times when we even sense that these expectations come from God. What do we do then?

The key is to learn to listen to God and to let our vision flow from there. This often involves developing some thick skin, while still keeping our sensitivity to the real pain and needs of people. Every effective leader must learn to live with the very people who frustrate them until they no longer do. The challenge is to stay balanced when criticized, to avoid taking the criticism personally yet to avoid becoming calloused or cynical. We are called to a paradox of personalities: sensitive but not easily offended, empathetic but not weak, flexible and yet filled with convictions.

That is all easier said than done, I know. In my own ministry, I still wrestle with these paradoxes. But here are a few leadership tips learned from scars:

1. Learn quickly what hills you will die on and which ones you must not.
2. Learn when to build bridges and when to draw lines, and don't get the two mixed up!
3. Learn when to confront and when to let it die and never bring it up again.
4. Learn that when you become a leader, you can never again get angry in public.

5. You can never defend yourself when a staff person or leader has been hurt by your comments. The best thing to do is to begin with the wash of repentance, even though it may not have been your doing. Repentance and forgiveness clean the wound. You cannot apply salve until you remove the grit which causes the pain.

WHAT'S WRONG WITH MY SHIRT?

One helpful way to find this balance is to break down the anatomy of an unwarranted expectation. At the core, many of the expectations, criticisms, and crises that we face originate from the same root cause, and they tend to be revealed in four main categories:

1. Stated: "I want you to do this, pastor."
2. Unstated: "You should have known I wanted you to do this, pastor."
3. Crisis: "I need you to do this for me now, pastor!"
4. Criticism: "You failed to meet my expectations, pastor."

The common theme running through all of these categories can be summed up best in a single word—*disappointment*. That's the root of all of these unwarranted expectations, criticisms, and crises. Someone wants help and is not getting the help they want, someone needs a problem solved and the problem is not going away, someone wants the church to minister to a certain type of person and it's not happening, someone is hurting and not getting any relief, someone is fearful and needs reassurance and comfort. It can all be summed up by the feeling of disappointment.

It may be helpful to put yourself in the position of one of your congregants for a moment. Many of them are facing challenges that are beyond their ability to control. They may be in deep pain. They may be wrestling with insecurity. And we shouldn't be surprised by any of this. We live in a fallen world, and it makes sense that if life is not working as it is supposed to work, people would turn to the church to relieve that sense of disappointment, to get help with their problems. Yet the reality is that neither a church nor a pastor can satisfy every person's disappointment. Not in an ultimate sense. There are some things that a pastor and a church can help with, but when that disappointment cannot be resolved to the person's satisfaction, I refer to these as unwarranted expectations.

I have known pastors who fall into this trap all too often. They wrongly believe that it is their job to make people happy. So they run themselves ragged trying to cater to the needs of people, or they push their staff to do this. And part of the problem is that as pastors we set ourselves up for failure. Wrongly, we try to position ourselves as the person to run to for help, when all along we need to be pointing people to Christ. In may sound strange, but there is a sense in which I can truthfully say that the church does not exist to help people, to solve their problems and alleviate their disappointments. Not ultimately, at least. The primary reason the church exists is to worship God and to point people to Christ, the ultimate solution to their problems. We are called to be the hands and feet of Christ, and I strongly believe that the Bible teaches us that the church is called to help people in practical ways. But our work should draw attention to the one who has saved us, the one who has solved our problems and given us hope in place of our disappointment. We point people to Christ, and we do ourselves a disservice any time we position ourselves as the ultimate answer to people's problems.

This new paradigm is a vision piece we must not only embrace but also help our people understand. In our well-meaning attempts to promote Christianity as the answer to everything, we sometimes overpromise when we present the gospel. We want churches to be happy places, so we end each service on a high note, giving the impression that happy feelings always come from church. Or we want to help everybody we meet, so we over-program our churches, attempting to offer ministries that cater to each subcategory of people we encounter. In the end we have churches filled with broad spec-trums of ministries operating at inefficient levels. We end up doing many things poorly when we should be doing fewer things well.

The answer to all of this is to strip down the gospel to its essence. The gospel is primarily about mankind getting right with a holy God. It is about God satisfying the requirements of his righteous-ness and holiness on behalf of sinful humans through the sacrifice of Jesus Christ. Though the kingdom of God exists both now and in the future, we must remember that there are many aspects of the kingdom of God that are still not realized on earth today, nor will they be until Christ returns. The gospel is not about our efforts to fix every social ill or to solve the problems of the world—it's about what God has done to make us right with him and how the cross and resurrection of Jesus change everything forever.

With that in mind, we may need to help people understand some of the following truths if we want to help them develop realistic, healthy expectations about the church and the role and abilities of those in leadership:

- The church will not always make you feel comfortable.
- The church will not be the answer to your every need.
- You will sometimes not like what happens at church.
- You might leave a service unhappy once in a while, particularly if you are seeing your sin in light of God's righteousness.
- If you are a single person, going to church will not guarantee you a spouse.
- Going to church will not guarantee that your children will not rebel.
- Going to church is not the answer to all your financial problems.
- You might not get along with everybody you meet at church.
- You might hate the color of the carpet, the taste of the coffee, and the shirt your pastor wears.

Again, the ultimate solution to the disappointments our people experience is pointing them to Christ, letting him be the Great Physician in their lives. Once we have done this, disappointment takes on a different nuance. Now, if people are disappointed, they are ultimately disappointed with God.

In other words, for those parents of a teenager crying in my office, so sad that their son is walking the wrong path, so desperate for help from the church, so expectant and even demanding that I intervene in their son's life, the one who has really disappointed them is God. They prayed about the situation. They begged God to intervene. So where is God? He is the one they are upset with.

When people come to us with their frustration, sharing their pain and disappointment with us, we need to dig beneath the layer of the immediate concern. When those parents are crying in my office (and I am crying with them), what they are ultimately expressing is that they are frustrated that God allows people to make bad choices — in this case, their son. The real work of a pastor, in this case, is not to try to solve their problems, particularly when pathways to immediate solutions have already been suggested and are not being heeded. Let me repeat that: the real work of a pastor is not to try to solve their problems. It is not to ratchet up the youth program, or to drop everything and help chase a rebellious teenage son, or to lock him in his room until he turns thirty. Rather, the real work of a pastor is to help give the parents a clearer sense of who God is, that God is good no matter what they are experiencing right now, that he desperately loves their son even to the point of allowing him to make poor choices. The real work of a pastor is to help people come to grips with God's goodness, even though we often do not understand his ways.

Or picture that same angry keyboardist, so frustrated that our church's worship team was not using him to his full potential, so expectant that he would regularly be given predominant roles in the worship service, so hurt his expectations were not being met — his real disappointment is with God. Why did God not intervene? Did the keyboardist not ask God to give him a greater ministry on the worship team? Why did God say no?

The wise church leader does not jump to cater to this man's demands and promise that he will be used more regularly on the worship team if that is not the best option. The wise leader will help this man see a righteous God contrasted with the prideful heart of man. Again, the ultimate work of a pastor is not to assuage this man's disappointment and solve his scheduling problem or his need to be in greater demand as a musician. It is to offer him a clearer sense of the character of God.

Let's do some work here. Picture the last time someone placed an unwarranted expectation on you as a leader, and perhaps the situation did not go so well. How might you have pointed the person to God instead, rather than trying to solve the problem yourself? Take a moment to answer the following questions:

◆ When the person came to me, he or she wanted:

_____

_____

_____

_____

◆ I tried to solve the problem by:

_____

_____

_____

_____

◆ But instead I could have pointed them to God by:

_____

_____

_____

_____

A MACEDONIAN CALL

Though we are not ultimately called to be the solution to other people's problems, the ones who provide hope for their disappointment in life, we are called to shepherd people along their journey. The various ministries of a church are designed to help people come closer to God. And whatever is done in a church, be it scheduling or counseling, it needs to be done excellently. While we are not called to be people's ultimate solutions, we are still called to point people to Jesus in an effective way.

With this in mind, sometimes very legitimate requests will come to you as a leader, and you will want to respond to them in timely and skillful ways. For instance, one of the ministries of the early church was to help widows in need (Acts 6:1). Note that in this particular case in Scripture, the church leaders wanted to spend more time praying and in the ministry of the Word, so they delegated this responsibility to a separate team of trusted leaders. Even though the primary leaders of the church could not be directly involved in meeting the need, the widows were being cared for. The ultimate solution in this case was to point the widows to Christ, but the church could play a very practical role as well. The immediate solution was to get food to these needy women. So the spiritual and the practical ministries intersected at this point.

As a twist on this subject, Acts 16:9 records the story of Paul receiving a vision of people in Macedonia asking him to come and minister to them. This call came from beyond the people; it came from God. If Paul had ignored this call, or had delegated it to a qualified leader, perhaps the needed ministry of planting churches in Macedonia would not have happened. So whenever people come to us with various requests, it is necessary that we make the distinction between the voice of God and the voice of man.

Discerning the voice of God is seldom easy. Pastors are apt to make more mistakes in this area when they are starting out in ministry. I said yes to more things in my earlier days than I do now. Hopefully, as I have grown older I have learned to discern God's voice better. But even after many years, this is no simple thing. In 1 Samuel 3, when the Lord calls Samuel as a young boy, even the seasoned priest Eli does not recognize the voice of God at first. God needs to call Samuel three times before Eli grasps that it is God talking. If this happened to Eli, as experienced as he was in serving the Lord, it can surely happen to us. Hearing God's voice and responding to his calling are never easy things to navigate through. Indeed, this in itself can be an important part of the sifting experience, growing in our dependence on God as he tests and refines us so that he can work through us.

When various calls come your way, my encouragement is to pray, wait on God, and say yes if you do not hear a clear no. If you don't say yes, then it will be more difficult to know if the answer is no. If you immediately say no without consulting God, then you will never know if a particular request actually came from God. And if you say yes, and it wasn't from God, then you are wiser in the end. Though it is fairly simple, I've found this to be a good, practical method of learning to discern the voice of God. Unless you hear a clear no, move ahead.

AN INVITATION TO LAMENT

I want to end this chapter by offering one very practical solution for when you encounter people's unwarranted expectations of you as a leader. This is not a popular solution, and I seldom hear it preached in churches today. But it is a biblical response. It's something we find modeled in the Psalms and in the ministry of the prophet Jeremiah and throughout much of the major and minor prophets of the Old Testament. We also see it in the life of Christ in his friendship with Peter and the other disciples.

A biblical response to disappointment, to the unanswered questions, the unresolved tension, the pain and suffering people bring to us is inviting them to lament. This means that when a person comes to you, and the problem cannot be solved, you point them to Jesus and invite them to honestly pour out their heart to the Lord. We know that God is the God of all comfort (2 Cor. 1:3). When we lament, we acknowledge that God is good and sovereign, yet life is not as we would like it to be. We find validation for our grieving in our lamentation. We learn that our emotions are permitted, that it is right to express them, even when those emotions include anger at injustice. The biblical form of lamenting allows people to feel and express the discomfort and disappointment they experience living in an imperfect world. When you invite people to lament, you are acknowledging that you, as a church leader, are with them in their journey, and you empathize with what they are going through. You do not try to cheer them up. You do not try to fix all their problems. You allow them to feel the hard truth, the raw emotion of the problem or circumstance. And you point them to God.

David cried out to God. So did Jesus, who prayed with "loud cryings and tears to the one who was able to save him from distress."

God himself did this with Job. After Job had lost his family, his health, his housing, his reputation, and his livelihood, God did not wipe away every tear, at least not at first. God did not try to make things all better for Job. God did not offer Job any solutions to his problems. God did not try to create a social program that would meet Job's needs. God did not crank up the ministries at the local church to help Job recover the things he had lost. God did not provide any clear-cut answers to what Job was going through.

God simply pointed Job to the realities of the moment: that Job was a man, and that God was God. He allowed Job to lament, to call out in distress, and then God pointed him to facts he could not fathom. It is perhaps the best example of pastoral ministry ever recorded.

REMEMBER
Seldom are your critics actually disappointed with you.

They are usually disappointed with themselves, their lives, or God.

You are simply a convenient target.

4

Cry Out to God

Muhammad Ali was once on an airliner ready for departure when the flight attendant noticed that the famous boxer had not fastened his seatbelt. "Excuse me sir, but would you please fasten your seatbelt?" she asked.

He replied, "My name is Muhammad Ali and I am Superman, and Superman don't need no seatbelt."

The flight attendant kindly asked him a second time, "I understand sir, but it is an FAA regulation that you fasten your seatbelt."

He shot back, "I said, my name is Muhammad Ali and I am Superman, and Superman don't need no seatbelt!"

The flight attendant excused herself and approached her supervisor and explained her plight. The supervisor said, "I'll take care of this," and walked back to the reluctant passenger. "Sir, you will need to buckle up!"

His reply was the same: "My name is Muhammad Ali and I am Superman, and Superman don't need no seatbelt!"

She quickly replied, "Yeah, but Superman don't need no airplane either! Now fasten your seatbelt!"

I readily admit I'm no Superman. But, just like Muhammad Ali, my beliefs about my own abilities weren't always based on reality. When I was laid low in the hospital after my surgery, I felt overwhelmingly spent, not only physically but emotionally. Often I wished for greater power, a type of energy that would enable me to jump out of bed and hurry back to the business of being a pastor. I was being sifted, and in that season, God's Spirit began to teach me another valuable lesson, a lesson about what true power really means.

I had always thought I was bulletproof. I had always considered myself invincible. But in my weakened condition I was finally forced to acknowledge that I was neither. I was finite and frail. Arriving at that conclusion, however, wasn't a simple process for me. It took brutal honesty, healthy introspection, and unfortunately, a heart attack. The secret to experiencing more of God's power in your life is first recognizing you are not that powerful after all. Let's take a closer look at what this important part of the sifting process means.

THE POWER OF WEAKNESS

The apostle Paul reminds us of a powerful truth in 2 Corinthians 12:9–10 in his response to God's words: " 'My grace is sufficient for you, for power is perfected in weakness.' Most gladly, therefore, I will rather boast about my weaknesses, so that the power of Christ may dwell in me ... for when I am weak, then I am strong."

Like many biblical truths, this is counterintuitive to most of us. Think about it—when we are weak, we are strong? It sounds nice, but what does this really mean?

I recall struggling through a season of ministry some years ago when everything seemed to be falling off the shelves. My family was in disarray, two board members were disillusioned, we had planted another church and many of our leaders left, and now we were low on funds. I prayed for God's power and kept motoring forward. But things began to go from bad to worse. Staff problems increased and my health began to suffer. Knowing that the ministry had to continue, I shook it off and regrouped. A few weeks passed, and then I could bear it no more. Ready to pack it in and call it quits, I did one last thing. I complained to God. "God! Why are you letting these things happen? Why are you letting me be so weak? I thought you were strong?" I remember hearing his reply to me: "The reason I cannot be strong for you is that you refuse to be weak."

Mark my words, Superman: there will be times in your life and ministry when, as David learned running from his enemies, the best thing to do is simply to cry out to God. Don't blame anyone else.

Don't play the victim card. Don't make excuses. Don't "suck it up" and try harder. Just cry out. That may be exactly what God wants from you—a cry for help, a dependent plea.

David, in his diary entry in Psalm 120:1, penned these words: "In my trouble I cried to the LORD, and He answered me." David was a powerful king of great influence, yet he cried out to God. Jesus himself modeled this posture, as we learn in the letter to the Hebrews. Read these poignant words from Hebrews 5:7: "In the days of His flesh, He offered up both prayers and supplications with loud crying and tears to the One able to save Him from death, and He was heard because of His piety." Here's a question: When was the last time you prayed with "loud crying and tears"? If it has been recently, know that you are in good company with men like David and Jesus. But also know that you're beginning to understand one of the most important keys to successful long-term ministry—that you're only as powerful as your dependence on God's strength. As I've been sifted, I've learned a lesson I call "the truth of passive power"—that God's power does not originate in weak, frail me. It passes *through* me, but it does not come *from* me.

- I used to pray, "I'm gonna live for God!" Now I pray, "God, come live through me."
- I used to pray, "I'm gonna work for God!" Now I pray, "God, come do your work through me."
- I used to pray, "I'm gonna serve God!" Now I pray, "God, please come and serve through me."

Let's unpack this idea and what it might look like in your life. Start by picturing the greatest challenge in front of you right now. In fact, take a moment to write it out. Complete the following sentence.

◤ The biggest specific challenge I face as a church leader right now is:

_____

_____

_____

_____

So, what are you doing about the challenge?

Are you trying to fix it?

If you said yes, you wouldn't be alone. And I won't berate you for trying. Undoubtedly, problem solving is part of pastoral ministry, and that's the way most of us are wired — if something is less than perfect, we want to make it better. I know how that goes. We fix and tweak and adjust and smooth and run around like beheaded chickens; sometimes a problem is fixed, but another problem jumps up to take its place. In our core, we believe that problem solving is the predominant paradigm — if we could only preach a better sermon, or plan a better outreach event, or have better worship music, or visit one more family in the church, then all would be well.

But let me invite you to suspend that problem for a moment and step away from the entire paradigm of problem solving for a while. What if you could just set that problem on the back burner for an hour and take a moment to — here it is — cry out to God? Let him know that without him, you can do nothing. Learn from King David, the one God called the "apple of his eye."

How do you do this? Simply get by yourself, and go to Jesus. No one needs to listen but God. You see, sometimes we don't know that Jesus is all we need until Jesus is all we've got. If we refuse to be weak, we never know what it means for Jesus to be strong. But don't wait until that reality strikes you. "Come to the end of your rope before you come to the end of your rope." In other words, don't wait until the pain of a crisis forces your hand. That doesn't take much faith; it takes only desperation.

I have an axiom I live by: We can teach what we know, but ultimately, we will reproduce what we are. If I want my congregation to be devoted to God's Word, what must I do? Teach on it? Yes and no. I must first be devoted to God's Word and prayer on a daily basis in my own life. And when devotion to God bleeds out of my toenails, then the people I serve will be infected positively by who I am more than by what I say. If I am serious about people loving their spouses, what must I do? Bring in special guest speakers on marriage? Yes and no. I must first deeply love my wife, Anna. I tell people the best thing I can do for my three children is to love their mother. And if I

GETTING PEOPLE TO LOVE GOD
Francis Chan

It's hard to be a church leader. We try so hard for people to love Jesus. And when they don't, we ask why — again and again. Like:

Why don't you people serve more?
Why don't you tithe more?
Why don't you love the people in your neighborhood more?
Why don't you share your faith?
Why do you keep looking at pornography?
Why don't you get along with each other better?
Why are there so many problems in your marriages?
Why are you pursuing all these material possessions?

Usually our commitment in response is to work harder. Maybe we can craft the perfect sermon, or perhaps through *this* counseling session we can say the perfect thing, or perhaps by building this program we will really get across what we want to communicate. (And sometimes we do need to work harder, for sure.)

But usually we need to realize a simple and yet complex truth. The ultimate work of a pastor is God's doing. We can't make people do anything. Paul's commitment in Ephesians 3:14–19 is to pray harder, and to pray for a specific thing: that people would know all the fullness of God, so that people can understand Christ's love for them.

That's a difficult concept to fully grasp. No matter how hard we work as church leaders, we will never be able to get people to love God. That work comes from God by the power of his Spirit. It's a supernatural exchange. God grants the love. If a person does not truly understand the depths of God's love, you will not be able to talk the person into it. This granting is something only God can do.

Imagine it this way. When my wife, Lisa, and I lived in Simi Valley, we often had people sharing our house with us. For some time, a young woman named Rochelle lived with us. She was single, and, like people in the Christian community are apt to do, Lisa and I tried as hard as we could to get Rochelle married off. Seriously — we introduced her to every single guy we could find. Rochelle didn't mind, and it proved fun for the whole family. Even our kids prayed that Rochelle would get married.

But no matter the extent of our efforts, there was no way that we could "make" any two young people fall in love with each other. Time and time again, Rochelle said no to the guys we introduced her to. Eventually, Rochelle fell in love all by herself. She's now married, and the couple is expecting a baby.

The same idea is at work here — you can't make anyone fall in love with Jesus, much as Lisa and I couldn't make Rochelle fall in love with a potential suitor. When it comes to Jesus and people, you can only make the introduction.

I can only tell you that God, the Creator of the world, the only God that matters, loves you deeply. He loves you more than your wife loves you, more than your kids, more than your mother or father, more than any boyfriend or girlfriend. God passionately loves you, so much so that he gave his son to die on the cross for you. It doesn't matter how messed up you are, how much you've rebelled against him, or even how indifferent you might be to matters of the cross; God still loves you deeply. While you were still a sinner, God loved you deeply. Who does this? Who gives his son to die in place of someone else? What an amazing God this is!

Yes, I can make this introduction, but nothing will happen until somehow, like Paul says, the Holy Spirit supernaturally gives a person the strength to know the love of Christ that surpasses knowledge. That phrase sounds almost contradictory — so read it again: God gives a person the strength to know a love that surpasses knowledge. He enables people to know something they can't know. You understand God's love in your inner being. Oh, how God loves us! And for people to understand this love, it comes only through prayer.

Prayer is the first and greatest work that we do.

want our precious saints to trust Jesus, what must I do? If I want our people to trust in God, what must I do?

It starts by coming to God in prayer with loud crying and tears.

FOUR WORDS THAT BEGAN A MIRACLE

If I told you I could give you four words that would start a miracle, would you be interested to know what they are? If I told you that there were four words that started the growth of New Hope in the early years which continues today, seventeen years later, what would you give to know that secret? Well, here they are for you, simple yet profound: "Will you help me?"

I know. You're thinking, "Man, that sounds corny." But seriously, when was the last time you sat with another leader and sincerely said those four words? You can't say them if you think you're Superman. You can't utter them if you think you're bulletproof, and you can't get them out if the practice of crying out to God is foreign to you. In the long run, only people who have experienced personal brokenness will know the value of these words.

I remember sitting with the district manager for Terminix Pest Treatment company. I asked him, "Will you help?" He is now one of our top pastors. I met with another man who ran an entertainment company for twenty-seven years, and I asked if he'd help me. I told him that the calling God gave us was far bigger than either of us. It was something that many would need to take ownership of. He is now our business administrator. I asked an award-winning high school conductor to help me, and he is now our creative director, leading our annual musical that runs more than twelve performances and is attended by thousands.

Of course, these four words won't be the answer to everything, but I've found that they begin the process of kingdom involvement. If people don't think you need their help, they won't offer it.

Recently we planted a new church and sent out one hundred people from the mother church to kick-start it. The new pastor came and asked for $55,000. "What for?" I pressed. "We need a sound system for our Sunday services, mics, and lights! We can't start without a sound system!"

I was keenly taken by his enthusiasm, but I pushed back anyway. "My suggestion is that you begin without a sound system at all." He was aghast that any new church plant should begin without a quality sound system. "I have often spoken to a hundred people without a microphone," I said. "At our staff meetings, which include a hundred people, do I use a mic?" "No," he replied.

"If you have a Santana-caliber sound system with a full lighting system, the congregation will sit back and figure you don't need their help or contribution," I explained. "Be excellent, but don't be afraid to be frail. Being meek does not mean you are weak. It may mean that you are being patient and giving people a chance to get involved. Take a special offering and let them be involved in the growth and improvement of the ministry. Ask them for their help. I promise you, it will be okay."

I am glad to report that he did just that. They took an offering and received more than enough to get started, and today, the church is dynamic and powerful with over one thousand people attending after just two years. All because this leader was willing to be weak, so God could be strong.

TURN AROUND MIRACLE

Recently, my alma mater, Eugene Bible College, called me. The president and chairman of the board met with me for dinner. "We're in deep weeds," he said. "We are speeding toward bankruptcy and our accreditation is in trouble. Will you help us?"

My first thought was that this was out of the question. I was pastoring our denomination's largest church, overseeing 114 others, writing books, and planting churches. Maybe they assumed I had some spare time that I was trying to fill. But in order to avoid vetoing anything that God wants to do with me, I told them I'd pray. As I did, I could feel an increasing pull toward this call, and later that week, I submitted it to our board of elders. They gave me permission to pursue it for a season, so I gave my consent and told the school I'd help for a season until it was turned around.

I guess I should have read the small print. One thing I wasn't aware of when I accepted was that they had been sinking into the red to the tune of $130,000 a month. One of my first meetings was with the school's banker, who told me in no uncertain terms that they would no longer extend credit to us. We were in deep, deep weeds! We needed to raise 2.6 million dollars to stay afloat, dodge the bankruptcy judge, and keep our accreditation. I remember several weeks later when our accountant informed me that we needed $240,000 by the following week or we couldn't pay salaries.

I smiled and said, "God will provide," then promptly went into my office and cried! We were knee-deep in red ink only to find out that it was red quicksand. If I didn't come up with the money, no one would get paid. There was no money tree in sight, but I had to raise some money right away. The jobs and families of our staff and faculty depended on it.

It takes a lot of humility to raise funds. Some like it. I hate it, but when your life depends on it, you put aside any thought of humiliation and you ask. After crying out to God, I knew I had to do something. Anything! The first man I met with was an old friend of mine. He was a dedicated saint and successful businessman. After explaining our predicament, I said, "Will you please help me?" (Okay, so I added another word to the four: *please*. I was desperate.)

Learn that phrase. It's key to any successful ministry.

"Will you please help me?"

After a brief conversation, he said he'd mull it over and call me back. The next day I received a phone call from him. All he said was, "Come on down and pick up a check." I cancelled all my appointments and drove over. He handed me a check for $300,000.

That was just the beginning. Over the next year, we raised over three million dollars to keep the school afloat. It is now well on its way to recovery, and though we have a long way to go yet, I know that New Hope Christian College will be strong and vital in the years to come, thanks to some generous people, a strong God, and a weak president.

Don't misunderstand my point. I am not espousing a welfare spirit or a poverty mentality. I am reminding us of the truth that Peter shares with us in his first epistle: "Humble yourselves under the mighty hand of God, that He may exalt you at the proper time" (1 Peter 5:6).

THE POSTURE OF STRENGTH

In order to posture ourselves for letting God be strong, there are three things we must do for ourselves. No one will force these things on us. These must be of our own choosing.

1. HUMBLE YOURSELF

I don't know if you've ever been humbled by God. I have. It is not fun. But God gives us a choice. We can choose to humble ourselves, or he will be happy to do it for us. It doesn't take me too long to decide on that one. I think I'll humble myself, thank you.

Do you know how to humble yourself? Are you willing to forego taking credit and passing it onto others instead? Or do you need to have your name on everything? Have you learned to say "I'm sorry"? Or do those words stick to the roof of your mouth like thick peanut butter?

Knowing how to humble yourself is a key to experiencing God being strong on your behalf. God opposes the proud, but he gives grace to the humble (James 4:6). Don't skip this one. You'll feel the pull that will wage war within you, but remember who you are opposing in your pride. It's a fight you will never win. Humility is the only path to receiving grace.

2. DISCIPLINE YOURSELF

Paul reminds the young pastor Timothy to "discipline yourself for the purpose of godliness; for bodily discipline is only of little profit, but godliness is profitable for all things, since it holds promise for the present life and also for the life to come" (1 Tim. 4:7–8).

That's a word we don't like much—*discipline*. But a friend once told me, "Wayne, there are two pains in life: the pain of discipline, or the pain of regret. You choose." Discipline is seldom fun, but the second thing you must learn to do is to discipline yourself. When you were young, others took on that responsibility: your mother, father, schoolteacher, even your older sister. But when you mature and come into your own, the direct discipline of others fades. This is especially true if success follows you, as you will find fewer people with the boldness or willingness to risk disciplining you. But success never means that we are above discipline. So what's the answer?

We must learn to discipline ourselves.

The Greek phrase used here is *gumnaze seauton*. *Gumnaze* is where we get our word *gymnasium*. This is actually a helpful picture for us today of what Paul intended. It's as if Paul is telling us to get back in the gym and work out. Develop the regimen that strengthens your muscles so that in the real race, you'll not fail because of an injury or a lack of preparedness. Paul instructs his young protégé to take the time in private to prepare for that which is public. And no one can do those preparations—your daily devotions, your time at home, your relationship with your spouse, your children, your thoughts—for you. Working on the things that are mostly unseen will directly affect that which is visible to everyone.

As we said earlier, it's the weight beneath the waterline that is most important.

3. ENCOURAGE YOURSELF

As you may have noticed, I find great encouragement in the story of David. He was often forgotten and despised, but he continually looked to God. First Samuel 30:6 (KJV) tells how once, "David was greatly distressed; for the people spake of stoning him, because the soul of all the people was grieved ... but David encouraged himself in the LORD his God."

Have you ever been forgotten? Perhaps your birthday came and went, and the ones who should have remembered didn't. Maybe you were overlooked in a group email, or someone forgot to invite you to a party. Or you lay ill in the hospital and no one visited.

We've all felt forgotten, with no one to encourage us. No one comes to pray for us, and there's no one to lift our spirit. We can sit there and blame others for their lack of sensitivity, or we can learn the art of encouraging ourselves! That one choice can mean the difference between fruitfulness and barrenness.

Do you ever talk to yourself? I do, sometimes. David did this a lot. He'd actually counsel himself, ask himself the tough questions, and he'd encourage himself. Read what he says in Psalm 42:11

(NIV): "Why, my soul, are you downcast? Why so disturbed within me? Put your hope in God, for I will yet praise him."

I love that verse! David talks to his discouragement and says, "Snap out of it. Get back to trusting God. Quit grumbling and start praising!" When all you have is Jesus, remember that you and Jesus make a majority. Cry out to him. He will never allow you to go through a valley without returning to you something that is of greater value. God never wastes a hurt.

REMEMBER
Sometimes you don't realize that Jesus is all you need until Jesus is all you've got!

PART TWO

home
work

Home: *noun*
The location where one's domestic affections
are centered.
Any place of residence or refuge.
 A principle base of operations or activities.

Every four years the Summer Olympic Games start with a long torch relay that spans multiple days and goes through various cities. This tradition originated in ancient Greece, where a fire was kept burning throughout the celebration of the Olympic Games. A torch was lit at the altar of Prometheus and was carried to the temple of Athena on the Acropolis. Then, during the Olympic Games, which were held in several cities, the same torch would light the flame in each location, signaling the start of the athletic competitions. The goal of this relay was not competition. It was protection—to carry the flame safely without extinguishing it, from one location to the next.

Imagine if a young, zealous runner in the torch relay, wanting to make a name for himself, falsely believed that speed was his only goal. He might sprint around a corner, thinking he is gaining an edge of a few seconds, when suddenly a gust of wind snuffs out the flame. Because he is making great headway, he continues the race. There is just one problem: he's now carrying an extinguished wick. Upon arrival, he proudly presents the charred torch stem to the elders of the city. How do you picture their reaction? I can imagine what the runner's next project will be: running back the way he came to renew the flame!

When it comes to our families, sadly enough, people in ministry are often like this runner carrying the flame. We continue pushing ahead toward the goal and often forget what's truly important in running the race. Because we are committed and zealous for God, we continue in the work of ministry, often with great speed and effort, carrying a flameless torch. We are still ministers, but our torches are darkened. The most important part of the race has been forgotten — those closest to us, our families, our loved ones, our children. Sadly, some will run the race for years with an extinguished wick.

How are you running the race right now? Is your flame burning dangerously low? Has it been extinguished?

In the next few chapters, we'll talk about running the race and keeping the flame of a healthy marriage and family life burning bright.

5

The Family Channel

When my father retired from the army, he purchased a ten-acre piece of undeveloped property in a little-known town called Trail. It is on the road to Tiller, if that helps you any. He purchased the property for seventy-five dollars an acre, so that might indicate how raw and untouched this mountainside landscape was. There was no water or roads, and the land desperately needed to be cleared. He had two sons with him at the time, my brother Gary and me—free labor! The soil was three parts shale and one part loam, so in order to plant a garden, we rigged up a four-by-eight sifting frame with a wire screen to sift dirt. We positioned the frame at an angle and threw shovelful after shovelful of dirt through the screen. The topsoil fell through the mesh, and the larger rocks and unusable clods of dirt stayed on top of the mesh to be discarded. After the shaking and sifting, one part went to the landfill and the other part to the garden.

It was hard, backbreaking work for two junior high kids, but the topsoil that it separated was a deep, beautiful brown, and the garden vegetables planted in this new soil grew to giant sizes. I loved the smell of the rich earth that would fall through my fingers, and I learned that growth happens best in sifted soil.

Do you want your patience to grow? That area of your life will be sifted. Want your finances to grow? That area of your life will be sifted. How about your people skills? That area of your life will be sifted. But what about your marriage, your family relationships? Do you want those to grow? Remember, nothing grows well until the soil has been sifted.

PROGRESS UNTO LIKENESS

Often our unstated, default goal in life is our leisure, but God's clear goal is likeness. He wants us to become like Christ. When we slumber, God shakes us to awaken our dozing faith. He has no trouble disturbing our comfortable equilibrium when we make stability our aim rather than growth.

I noticed something intriguing about my children when they were just learning to walk. At ten months old, my young son, Aaron, struggled to stand, and finally after multiple collapses he steadied his shaky legs and stood. My wife and I clapped, cheered, and took pictures. But the young tyke refused to be satisfied with mere standing up. He now wanted to walk.

The first step Aaron had to take was being willing to risk his current stability. Even as a young child, he intuitively knew that in order to walk, he had to give up the steadiness he had from grasping the table or the couch. He had to disturb his equilibrium, test his balance. He shifted his weight to one leg, lifted the other, leaned forward until he was off balance, then caught himself by putting his weightless foot in front of the other. And when he steadied himself, we clapped. His first step! There was progress — growth! But Aaron wasn't satisfied. Again, he intentionally disturbed his equilibrium and shifted his weight. Step two! He did this, again and again, until he was taking step after step, all because he chose to disturb his comfort for the sake of advancement.

The path to progress follows the same principle that we all learned as toddlers. Toddlers want to walk; they see others walking, and they want to grow. This is the secret to likeness. We grow because we are willing to change — to risk what we have — rather than settling for the status quo. In life, we won't get what we desire. We will receive what we settle for. So what have you settled for in your marriage? What have you settled for in your family? Have you settled for a marriage that is average? Have you assented to one that is acceptable rather than exceptional?

UNBELIEVABLE LOVE
Francis Chan

As leaders, too often we approach God with the attitude that we're doing amazing things for him. "Well, God, look what I'm doing for you — I'm planting a church. I'm making real sacrifices for you. I'm doing incredible works for you." We struggle to keep up an image of a perfect servant, one who's dutifully performing for God. Practically, we still believe following Jesus is about following a list of rules. We reduce the gospel to a system of dos and don'ts, a means of earning ourselves into God's favor.

But this is not the way of God. God has always been about love. The gospel is not about religion; it's not something we earn or deserve. It is the most romantic love story you will ever hear. It's about a Creator who is so filled with love toward mankind that he points to each person and says, "You, I want you. I want to stick a ring on your finger. I'm crazy about you." And I have to say, there's nothing quite like the family to illustrate just how God loves us.

At one of the last weddings I performed, the bride was a middle-aged woman, Jean, who has a twenty-eight-year-old special-needs daughter named April, who was the flower girl at the wedding.

Jean is normally a woman very filled with joy. Yet in the weeks before the ceremony, during the pre-marital counseling sessions, she told me how she couldn't believe she was going to get married at last. Anytime she looked at her fiancé, Rick, self-doubts filled her mind — not about him, but about herself. She would whisper to her fiancé, "I just can't believe it. Are you sure you want to marry me? I'm old. I'm wrinkled." And Rick would whisper back, "Nah, those lines are like dimples to me. You're beautiful."

Here's the clincher. The day of the ceremony, everything was wonderful and perfect. Then right in the middle of the ceremony came a big surprise. After the vows were taken, I explained that Rick had also bought a ring for April, Jean's daughter, because Rick wanted April to know that he was also adopting her as his very own. Rick was committing himself to her as a father.

The moment I announced it, April screamed with joy and ran toward Rick, her brand new father. She hugged him, crying, screaming, saying over and over, "I love you, I love you, I love you!" And Rick hugged her right back. April could not believe Rick was making a commitment not only to her mother but to her too.

Rick placed the ring on April's finger. Everyone was bawling by then, including me, and I stopped the ceremony right then and there and explained how a clear picture of God's love was just portrayed. The Bible says that God looks upon us as his bride. Rick took Jean to be his bride, and she couldn't believe it. She wondered, "Are you sure you really want me?" and Rick said to her, "Are you kidding? Yes, I want you! Yes, I love you! And I love all that comes with you."

That's a picture of us and God. We look at ourselves and wonder if God loves us. "God, are you sure you want me? I've made such a mess of my life." And God says, "Yes, I want you! Yes, I love you, just like my bride."

But the Bible also uses another analogy. It says that God is a father to the fatherless. He adopts us as his children. You and I are invited to be like April in saying, "Are you kidding me? There is no way! I can't believe you're taking me as your child."

But it's true! And that's the type of emotion, joy, and unbelievable sense of awe and wonder that we can have when we approach God. "God, I can't believe this — you love me! You're placing the ring on my finger, for better or worse."

And that's one reason families are so important — your own family, as well as families in the church. They help us see God in ways we never could otherwise.

So what is God saying to you through your family, your marriage? How are you seeing his love for you today through them?

GREATEST JOY, GREATEST FEAR

During a breakout session at a recent leadership conference, I met with about twenty young leaders under the age of forty, all from churches of more than three thousand members. These were hard-hitting young leaders, dynamic and gifted. In that session, we went around the room sharing joys and sorrows, until we came to one leader who is known quite well in the States and perceived as successful in the pastorate. I'm not exactly sure what everyone else was expecting to hear, perhaps some story of how God was using his church mightily, but what he said was a testament to vulnerability and authenticity. It stopped many of us cold.

"My greatest fear," said the leader, "is that my kids will grow up hating God because of me."

There was so much power in that simple statement and so much genuine concern and fear. His fear was not only that his children would be indifferent; the fear was that his children would be antagonistic toward God. And he placed the blame not on the church or on the surrounding secular culture or even on his children's individual free wills but on himself. "Because of me," he said, "my children may actually hate God." Those words tore at my soul, as I think they did for everyone else in that room.

As more of the story came out, this leader expressed how he was so driven by the cause of ministry that he was forsaking the needs of his family. The pattern of living he had chosen was catching up to him, and he was worried, very worried. If he continued to follow this pattern, he saw only disaster ahead.

His story is more common than we'd like to think. Young leaders, often without realizing it, are prone to place far greater value on their ministries than on their family and marriage. But in actuality, family and marriage are in the same sphere as pastoral ministry. They are so closely intertwined, they truly cannot be separated. We would be wrong to conclude that every time a child of a Christian leader rebels it is the fault of the parent. We know that even the perfect Father has rebellious children. We also know that it is no guarantee that the children of Christian leaders will also walk with God. This knowledge should encourage us to increase the priority we place on our homes. We cannot assume that our own house is in order, neglecting our family for the sake of the ministry. Our families *are* our ministry.

One of the main reasons I can stand at the podium each weekend and preach is because of my family. Paul reminds us of that goal in 1 Timothy 3:4, saying a ministry leader "must be one who manages his own household well, keeping his children under control with all dignity (but if a man does not know how to manage his own household, how will he take care of the church of God?)."

Paul asks a great question here, and he puts the responsibility for household management on the leader. Each of us must realize that we are only as busy as we choose to be. Think of it this way: the darkest place on a lighthouse is its base. But no one is forcing us to neglect the base of our lighthouse. No one is forcing us to neglect our families. We must learn to take responsibility for leading our families in righteousness as part of our commitment to ministry in the church.

But how can this be done? With the multitude of responsibilities a ministry leader faces, how do you effectively prioritize your ministry to your family?

THE MOVING FULCRUM

Imagine a fulcrum, that point where a lever balances, like the middle of a seesaw. The fulcrum is the center point of the machine, critical to keeping things, well, balanced! In your life, that fulcrum is your heart.

Now imagine the opposite ends of your seesaw heart. At one end is your family, at the other, your church ministry. Perhaps you feel some tension in doing this. You may ask yourself, "Where does family begin and ministry end?" And that's my point. Neither ministry nor family begins where the other ends. They're often one and the same. They are both integrated parts of your life, making up the same seesaw. Your life is your ministry, your commitment to serving the church is your ministry, and your family is also your ministry. These are not disjointed callings. They are all part of the same call, and the movement of your attention, your heart, will reveal the balance point.

We all know that life is never static. We never live in a 50/50 balance. We're always on the move, so balancing life with family, self, and ministry to others will require a moving fulcrum. There are some weeks when the attention I give to ministry in relation to the attention I give my family is more like 70/30, and there are other times when it might be 90 percent family and 10 percent ministry. It all depends on what is going on, where the needs are, what God is doing at that time. Nothing is ever a stable 50/50, which is why it's hard to lay down rules and guidelines in this area. As soon as you create them, they must be broken.

There will be times when the Holy Spirit sees a storm cloud forming over your marriage. In order to move you to put energy in that direction, he will put his finger on that part of your life and push. You'll lurch and feel like your life is out of balance. You can ignore this or try to run from it, but if you ignore it for too long, you will soon live with the consequences of a lopsided marriage and an off-balance relationship.

In order to cooperate with his Spirit, you must learn to move your heart (the fulcrum) toward him in order to balance it out. For a season, move closer to your family — spend more time, more attention, more of your focus, more money, more of whatever it takes! By shifting focus, you may feel like an off-centered seesaw, but you'll be balanced. This is what the Bible commonly calls "following the leading of the Holy Spirit." And that is the underlying principle of the fulcrum. As you move your heart closer to what the Holy Spirit is doing, you will have a life that is always moving, always ebbing and flowing, and you will be able to stay balanced.

Just don't assume that you'll ever arrive at the point of perfect balance and remain there. As soon as you get to that place, God will lift his hand and say, "Okay, your marriage is much better. Now I want you to work on your finances." And you'll feel the balance shift with a weight brought to that area of your life. When that takes place, the only way forward is to move your fulcrum in the direction he is moving and pay attention to his leading until he says otherwise. Again, the balance we seek is not for our comfort or leisure; it is constantly moving because it is part of the sifting process, the means God uses to help us grow into the likeness of Christ.

Incidentally, the *shekinah* glory of God in the Old Testament was expressed as a pillar of fire by night and a cloud by day. It was the presence of God that led the children of Israel through the desert. The Hebrew word for glory is *kabod*, which literally translated means "weight." In other words, it is the weight of God that we follow, and as we do, he leads us through the wilderness seasons of our lives and into his full promises for our future. As God's weight shifts, the seesaw of our lives will move, leaving us feeling unbalanced yet again. As we move the fulcrum, pursuing the glory of God, we grow and change into the likeness of his glory, becoming more and more like Jesus.

PLUGGING THEM IN

In order to keep ministry and family from separating into two distinct worlds, I aim to plug my family into my hip pocket. In other words, I purposely try to merge the worlds of family and ministry. When we pioneered our second church, I clearly remember my youngest laying in a bassinet while we set up for services. I didn't shield my family from the ministry. I blended them right in. Ministry is an amazing adventure, and I wanted to share that with my whole family. We were in it together!

I remember approaching our church board with a proposal to take one of my children or my wife with me each time I traveled for ministry. Of course, this would cost another airfare, so I asked permission from the board to include my wife's travel expenses in the budget. One of them replied, "Why are you taking your wife? Why don't you take a member of the church?"

"My wife *is* a member of our church," I pointed out.

"Yes, but you should take an elder or staff person. You see, this is ministry, not family time," they said.

I firmly but gently replied, "Yes, but I can still minister effectively while she's there. And here's why I'd really like to take her: If an elder goes bad, I will feel horrible, but the church will keep going. If a staff person buckles, we let him go and the church continues. But if my wife goes awry, I don't keep going with the church. I'm done!" The board understood, and for years I traveled, not always, but often, with my wife or another member of my family.

My son Aaron has traveled all around the world with me, and today he is a pastor of a thriving work in Hawaii. Ministry became a part of his life and it was seen as an adventure, a journey with the Lord we took together, rather than something in tension with the family. My two daughters love Jesus and live God-glorifying lives, and my wife, after thirty-eight years of marriage, still thinks I'm awesome. (I think that's what she'd say, anyway.)

THINK MORE LIKE A FARMER

The book of Ecclesiastes reminds us of a powerful truth: "To everything there is a season, and a time to every purpose under the heaven" (Eccl. 3:1 KJV). Farmers need to pay close attention to the seasons. Springtime is the most active time, when a farmer must work around the clock preparing the ground, planting seed. He has to insure that his equipment is in tip-top shape, for he has but a small window of time for planting and harvesting his crop before the season changes into winter.

Those who live in cities don't need to pay attention to the seasons in this way. Metropolitan workers typically do the same things year round, and they get a paycheck after a forty-hour-a-week job, rain or shine. But farmers must live differently. During the planting season, they don't take a vacation. They don't visit relatives or plan a trip. The farmer plants his fields. And during the haying season, the farmer doesn't paint his fence. He doesn't repair roofs or repair gutters. He bales hay. The farmer watches for a spell of sunshine and pays close attention to the rains. Then he works from dawn to dusk.

One of the difficulties we face in our modern age is that we have lost this sense of the seasons. Those who farm recognize that priorities change with the seasons. They understand that there are natural rhythms to life, that things change and we must change with them if we want to grow, survive, and thrive. The modern age can dull us to the natural rhythms of life, and as a result, we ignore the changing seasons of life and our priorities begin to slip out of balance. We must learn to pay attention to seasons because the Holy Spirit moves in seasons, and an essential part of growing into the likeness of Christ is learning to recognize what season we are in. So what season are you in right now?

- ◆ A family season?
- ◆ A season for personal and emotional health?
- ◆ A season for ministry concentration?
- ◆ A season to focus on one of your children or your spouse?
- ◆ A season for organizing your life?
- ◆ A season to renew certain relationships?
- ◆ A season of building new leaders?

You will need to discern the times and seasons, alert your family, and together work in tandem with the Spirit of God. Take a few moments to think through and answer the following questions.

◤ What season are you in now? Is it a season of personal health? Maybe it is one where you are to deepen your personal devotion or ratchet back to Jesus Christ. Write down what season you think you are in and what the Holy Spirit is emphasizing that you must focus your attention on:

_____

_____

_____

_____

◤ What seasons have you missed in the past? Has there been a time when the Holy Spirit highlighted something or someone and you didn't pay attention?

_____

_____

_____

_____

THE TOP OF YOUR LIST?

1 Timothy 3 indicates that a leader's household must be properly managed. This means that, biblically speaking, a leader cannot have a successful ministry if his home life is in ruins. It might be helpful to examine some models of prioritizing. Listed below are the priorities I once lived by. Regardless of what I taught, the way I lived in the beginning was shaped by these unbalanced priorities:

1. God
2. Ministry
3. Family
4. Self

God and ministry were numbers one and two, and since God and ministry were closely combined in my mind, it often meant that the church took all my time. Church work was all-encompassing for me, and, I hate to admit it, in many senses I viewed my family as a necessary evil. Having a family took too much time away from the church. The responsibilities of caring for my family often felt like a burden to me—a nice burden, mind you. But this nagging voice often hissed, "You would have been so much more effective if you weren't married," or, "You can always postpone playing catch with your son. Let's face it, you've got an important meeting that can't wait."

These voices were deeply wrong on many levels. I have since learned that the exact opposite is true. A church leader's spouse and family can help provide the stability, sanity, and balance in a leader's life. It was after I experienced a profound burnout that I restructured my thinking and my life. I have come to realize that my priorities are now the following:

1. God
2. Self
3. Spouse
4. Family
5. Ministry

This may not look as you imagine it should, but let me take a moment to unpack this list. Too often, our personal lives are like churches that develop a mission statement and then file it away in a drawer somewhere. The exercise complete, it's now back to business as usual.

GOD

We all probably agree that we must prioritize God first because everything must flow from our relationship with Jesus. It doesn't matter if you are a pastor or a leader in the church, no one can grow and experience health in their life if this relationship is not a priority. So my daily devotions are prioritized as an essential aspect of my growth in Christ. The best thing I can do for my wife, Anna, and my children is to love Jesus first because when they see that Jesus is always first, they are confident that our family will be fine. This is not to suggest that our life will be perfect and free from mistakes or without problems. But my family can be confident that even though sins can easily entangle me, I will always be open to correction because the Spirit of God has clear and regular access to my soul.

If we place ministry first, perhaps driven by a secret need to be known and loved or valued, then we are unbalanced. We are like a wheel whose hub is off center: the car lopes and surges no matter how finely tuned the engine is. Following Jesus first balances our perspective. If he is not at the center, we may be convinced that we are right about something when, in fact, we are dead wrong. We will think we are on track, but our GPS will be miscalculating, blocked from the satellite signal. Jesus recalibrates the map and balances the way we see life.

SELF

I put myself second because I've come to understand that if my health isn't stable, nothing else functions well. I have learned this the hard way. Scripture encourages us to love our neighbors as ourselves (Mark 12:31), and there has been much debate about what this passage means and doesn't mean. Certainly, there is a sense in which self-love can be harmful to a person if he selfishly exalts himself above others or God. But we should also recognize that in this passage Jesus tells us to love others in the same way that we love ourselves. In the past, I didn't love myself in a healthy way. I gave myself to serving others, continually making my own health and welfare my lowest priority. In many ways,

I was relying on my own strength to empower this. I intentionally diminished myself, which seemed noble, but I was dead wrong. My health, my weight, and my energy suffered. Ultimately, my life was at risk. I have learned that the way I treat myself will ultimately affect the way I treat others. If I don't learn to love myself in a way that is healthy, a way that honors God, I will struggle to love others in this way.

SPOUSE

I list my spouse third now, intentionally ahead of my children, because it actually bolsters my children's confidence when they see that my spouse is prioritized. The secret to a healthy marriage is to fall in love, again and again, and always with the same person. When my children see me honoring their mom, it gives them a great sense of stability, and they can get on with their development without fearing a fractured family or a distant dad.

One day, it will be just Anna and me again. No kids, no church, no daily ministry meetings. One day, I will clean out my desk and walk out of the office, and when I do, I will walk out of one thing and into another. If my marriage is unhealthy, when I walk out of the office, what do I walk into? A healthy relationship with my spouse is of utmost importance to my future joy.

FAMILY

My family ranks fourth. I am the only dad my children will ever have. Other pastors will come along for our congregations, but no other dads will come along for my kids. Again, according to 1 Timothy 3, one of the main reasons I can stand at the pulpit is because my marriage and family are doing well. If I end up nondescript in ministry success, but my family is in love with Jesus because their dad modeled a vibrant faith, I will be delighted. Today, all my children are in love with Jesus in sincere ways, and my grandchildren are following in the footsteps of a genuine faith. There is no greater joy than this.

MINISTRY

Ministry ranks fifth. It's important but not the be-all and end-all of life. Ministry cannot be allowed to consume a leader. In ministry circles, we often sacrifice our marriages and families on the altar of ministry success. But ranking ministry as number five does not mean it is unimportant. By no means! It simply means that it becomes increasingly important only as the other foundational pieces are in place first. Without a foundation, a building will sag. Proper footings are crucial, but prioritizing the quality of foundation in no way diminishes the importance of the building that has been planned. You just can't compromise on what holds the building up, and like the keel and ballast of a sailboat, what is beneath the soil is as important, if not more, as what is seen above it.

What I have learned the hard way through my own seasons of sifting is that the traditional paradigms of priority settings are faulty. And in some ways, the lists I've just presented to you do not convey the real picture. The reality, as we emphasized earlier, is that following Jesus and pursuing your calling as his disciple is never a static undertaking. As the Holy Spirit leads you, move accordingly. At times, you will need to devote 100 percent of your time, energy, and effort to church ministry. At other times, you will need to devote 100 percent of your time, energy, and effort to your family. Everything revolves around the leading of the Holy Spirit, who "guides you into all truth." In that sense, he will always be the first priority—that's the one thing that will never change. The wise leader needs to learn to identify times and seasons and adjust accordingly, sometimes shifting the emphasis to ministry, sometimes shifting the attention to family. My encouragement is to move the fulcrum of your heart to the area that needs attention, within the parameters of the list above. In other words, while priority lists like these are helpful, they are only a guide to shape our focus and clarify our desires; they aren't a rulebook to determine what we should do in every season of life.

A GOOD DAY FISHING

Once I was in a season of family, yet it was also a time when the church was thriving. Many new people were joining the congregation. We were in our first church in the sleepy town of Hilo, Hawaii, with a population of thirty-six thousand. The church had grown to nearly two thousand people, something that was unprecedented in that area; the next largest church was three hundred people. We were seeing signs that God was at work all around us. Our days were filled with follow up, leadership training, and management.

But the Holy Spirit chose that time to put his finger on my family, especially on my relationship with my sixth-grade son, Aaron. At the time, I didn't know exactly why he put his emphasis on Aaron, but I knew that I needed to spend time with him. It might have been something brewing in my son's heart, or possibly God knew that he would be challenged in the days to come and would require confidence in his father's love and attention.

That's how sifting goes. You often won't know the why. You will be shown only the what.

It was a school day, but I loaded up our little nine-foot boat with some lunch and fishing poles. I hooked it onto my car and drove to his school. I explained to the principal that I needed to spend time with Aaron, and thankfully he understood. I went to Aaron's classroom and, with a note from the principal, Aaron packed up his little backpack. Hand in hand, we left the room and walked down the hall.

"Where we going, Dad?" he inquired.

"We're going fishing!" I said. He let out a whoop that made me quicken my step before the principal changed his mind.

We spent the whole afternoon in the bay fishing. We ate lunch together. We talked and laughed. And today, if you ask him, he still remembers the day when his dad pulled him out of class to go fishing. It was a season for me to invest in my family, and it may not be until I get to heaven that the Lord will unpack the reason why things were that way, but I am convinced that my life, my ministry, and my family would be different today if I hadn't moved my fulcrum toward the leading of the Holy Spirit on that day, years ago.

REMEMBER
Never sacrifice your marriage or family on the altar of ministry.

6

Rest, Sabbath, Drive

There's an old rabbinical saying that never ceases to challenge me. "God will one day hold us each accountable for all the things he created for us to enjoy but we refused to do so."

Do you ever have days that seem far too busy to enjoy?

Picture one now: Up at 5:00 a.m., rise and shine, shower, you're out the door to a breakfast meeting. You run hard all day long; the schedule is crammed with an endless series of phone calls, meetings, planning blocks, study times, counseling sessions. You grab a quick bite for lunch. Dinner is on the run. Another meeting is scheduled for evening. You commute home in darkness and collapse into bed at midnight, only to get up at 5:00 a.m. again, ready for another day just like it.

What happens when you have a month like that?

Or a year like that?

Or ten years like that?

Or a lifetime like that?

I know what it is like to be too busy. As I write this, I am between flights, sitting at the executive lounge in the airport in San Francisco. I've just come from our church in Hawaii and I'm heading to my responsibilities at the college in Eugene, Oregon. I'm on the phone with my editor and we're talking through the flow and content for this very chapter. It's 3:45 p.m. and I've just landed. My next flight boards at 4:45 p.m., which means I have slightly less than an hour for this meeting, and then I'm onto the next thing.

I like my editor just fine, and the meeting goes smoothly, but frankly, my brain is tired, and the content is coming more slowly than I'd like. In the past two-and-a-half weeks in Hawaii I've spoken fourteen times. When I get to the college, I need to hit the ground running. I remind myself, silently, that my schedule at this moment is not conducive to operating at a sustainable pace. Sometimes in ministry the pace needs to be ramped up like this. But, usually, if I want to thrive and survive with joy, something will need to give, and I will need to proceed more slowly, with greater spaces of margin deliberately built into my life.

Fortunately, I've learned a bit about the art of self-correcting. Oh, I am still learning, mind you, but one of the greatest lessons in life is finding the edges of your plate. You see, everyone's plate is a different size. Some can multitask much better than others and handle much more than others can, but if you never find the edges, you'll never know what you could have accomplished. So there is some value in pushing yourself, but the key is learning to pull back and self-correct, especially when you hit the rumble strips. Many highways have rumble strips, uneven strips pressed into the pavement that vibrate the fillings of your teeth right out of your gums when dozing drivers drift into them. You are now fully awake, and you correct your course. If for some reason you choose to ignore the rumble strips, the next encounter will be with the guardrails.

When you get near the edges of your plate, you will feel the rumble strip. You can ignore it, but only to your own peril. The best discipline of all is the ability to self-correct so you won't require the guardrails. Now when I feel the rumbling that warns me that I've headed off the road, about to crash and burn, I schedule rest—not after I am exhausted, but just before I get there.

I remember once I was about to embark on a grueling canoe race thirty-one miles around the cape of Kauai. It would take us nearly four hours to complete. In order to keep our energy up, we had individual pouches of power gels taped to the side gunnels of our canoe, and we were to consume one every hour. Next to us were water bags with a small hose from which we were instructed to swallow three gulps every fifteen minutes. I remember asking my coach, "But what if I'm not thirsty?" He quickly reiterated, "Every fifteen minutes, three big gulps." I pressed, "But why don't I just drink when I am thirsty?" He spoke quietly but firmly, a lesson I have never forgotten: "If you wait to drink until you're thirsty, you're too late. Your body is already dehydrated. You must drink before you get there!"

I've learned how to drive myself hard, how to push myself to my limits after learning my limits, and how to build in a time for rest before I need it. I'm much better than I used to be at taking regular time off for restoration, recharging, and fun. This upcoming summer, for instance, numerous requests have come to me for speaking engagements and strategy sessions, but I've said no to 80 percent of them. There were many great opportunities for ministry available, but I knew it would be wisest in the long run if I simply said no. This summer I want to spend time with my family and do some more writing. Those are my priorities. Those ministry opportunities will need to go to someone else.

What is your schedule like? Do you find yourself constantly running from one activity to another? Do you feel tired most days, unsure of what to prioritize? Or do you know what it means to operate at a sustainable pace? Have you found the vital balance between work and rest, between Sabbath and drive?

OUR WELL-INTENTIONED DRIVING

This is a subject that Larry, Francis, and I have discussed at length, and we have all noticed that by nature, ministry leaders are hard-chargers. This character trait seems to be hardwired into us. It doesn't matter what task we tackle, we tend to be an intense bunch. We've all seen various ways in which this trait is expressed in the lives of leaders we personally know:

- We've been out with successful ministry leaders playing golf, and they do not like to lose.
- We've done home projects with them like building a fence or installing a new lawn, and they do not like to stop for coffee breaks.

◆ We've been in meetings with ministry leaders, and they want action and results.

Often this trait can be good—whatever job needs doing, hard-chargers get the job done. But often this can also be detrimental. Hard-chargers can walk over people, ignore valuable processes, or burn themselves out. There are some in leadership who are so pressed they can't even take time to eat. Before we deconstruct this trait in depth, let's look at some of the positive reasons why leaders act this way.

There is a noble intent behind much of this. First, ministry pioneers are tasked with the incredible responsibility of creating situations in which people can gather to journey closer to Christ. The job of pastoral ministry, by definition, has eternal consequences. We're not simply digging ditches here, or fixing teeth, or driving a bus, or putting a basketball into a hoop—although all those professions can be noble undertakings. We are handling people's lives, the very words of God, and how they intersect. It's normal for a church planter to sense a mandate that originates in eternity. We *must* do this, we believe, because God calls us to this work and it has eternal consequences. That's a serious responsibility, and it calls for intentional, serious action. We are driven because the stakes are so high.

Second, ministry pioneers need to be entrepreneurial by nature in order to succeed. Starting a new ministry, or even entering into a new ministry, can be a lot like starting a business, and nobody who starts a business succeeds by sitting around all day twiddling his thumbs. An entrepreneur takes risks and works hard. Those are the unavoidable foundations of success. None of us entered the world of church planting because we wanted a quiet, safe kind of life. We wanted purpose and consequence, with all the highs and lows that come along with it. We embraced the challenge of rigorous living. In the words of Teddy Roosevelt, "Far better is it to dare mighty things, to win glorious triumphs, even though checkered by failure ... than to rank with those poor spirits who neither enjoy nor suffer much, because they live in a gray twilight that knows not victory nor defeat."

We do what we do in the spirit and example of Jesus Christ, who risked leaving heaven, who risked his reputation, who left his comfort and security for the sake of the kingdom, and who called rugged and powerful disciples to him by uttering these gutsy words, "Whoever wants to be my disciple must deny themselves and take up their cross daily and follow me" (Luke 9:23 NIV).

Third, ministry pioneers pursue noble intents but are not armed with unlimited resources. In the eyes of God, a church leader has access to the proverbial cattle on a thousand hills (Ps. 50:10). Indeed, there is no limit to God's resources. But church leadership is not like an investment startup where a young entrepreneur approaches a bank or a group of investors and begins a task with two million dollars in hand. Most church leaders, particularly those planting a new church, are hard-pressed to hire adequate staff and secure adequate meeting rooms. In this line of work, employees are not driving Cadillacs, nor do they hope to. It's the non-profit sector, and even when the enterprise is up and running, a church leader must rely heavily on volunteers to keep the endeavor successfully operating. Volunteers can sometimes be difficult to manage, and, as such, a leader is prone to pick up the slack, sighing and grumbling to himself things like, "If you want anything done right, you need to do it yourself." A church pioneer operates within the framework of social action, not financial gain.

Thus, it is normal and natural for a church leader to be hard-driving. Indeed, this sort of hard-driving mentality is expected and even required to succeed in this line of calling. Nevertheless, we must ask ourselves a larger question: If our hard-charging is not tempered by balance, where will this lead us? Is hard-charging all that's required of us, or is it something that springs from a wiser approach to life?

CASE STUDIES

Let me offer a few stories of church leaders we know and the schedules they've kept. Examine the stories with an eye to health. Ask yourself if their actions were wise, if their patterns of living and ministry were sustainable, even what you might have done in a similar situation. The names and a few of the details have been changed, but all the stories are true.

PLANTING IN A NEEDY AREA

David came to church planting after six years as a college minister. His work was in a downtrodden area of his city, and the church quickly grew from a core team of about twenty to a congregation of about one hundred and twenty. His church grew mostly from the marginalized people who wouldn't normally come to church—drug and alcohol addicts, people living homosexually, welfare mothers, a few mentally handicapped and special needs people, and a few David described as "a sweet and troubled collection of elderly oddballs."

At first, the church enjoyed a climate where vitality and excitement were abundant. David's core members stayed on, and together they were able to care for the needs of the growing congregation. Discipleship groups started. A recovery class was always full. They opened the church building all hours and staffed it around the clock to provide a sheltering ministry for the homeless. David noted that when people are radically saved, a lot of radical joy can result. Worship services were often long and loud, filled with exuberant expressions of genuine gratitude to God.

One by one, however, David's core team began to tire and then drop out. A variety of reasons were cited, but the predominant theme was fatigue. The team was, quite simply, exhausted. The new congregation was growing, but the rate of incoming leaders didn't match the growth. It took too much work to staff the homeless shelter, and it took a certain kind of leader too—it was work that required sensitivity, fearlessness, and even a robust physical strength. Volunteers sometimes faced altercations and confrontations with unruly patrons. Sometimes the police would need to be called. The ministry was vibrant, but it was pure and simple hard work.

Despite fewer volunteers, the ministry kept increasing. Over time, David saw the need for life-skills classes, a counseling center, and a day care. Pretty soon he was at the church building around the clock as well. He never took a day off. He taught 90 percent of the classes. He shouldered the entire counseling load. On Sundays he preached twice and led the music.

Three years later he found himself in the hospital. A doctor did a thorough examination and handed down a simple ultimatum: "You're burned out. Get some rest."

BIVOCATIONAL CHURCH PLANTING

Brandon felt a strong urge to plant a church when he was half-way through seminary. The work of the gospel was too important to wait until graduation, he believed. Besides, he was young and fit. His wife was on board with the plan. She worked outside the house only part time, and her mother, who lived just down the street, was able to watch the couple's two young daughters during the times she needed to be at work. Brandon worked part time for a photography studio, which offered him flexible hours. Surely he could juggle all of his responsibilities at once. His was a generation of strong multitaskers. So he began the plant.

He started his church in his city's college district, with a handful of families from the seminary joining the work. They met in a house for the first month then rented the seminary's chapel. Brandon was a gifted speaker and Bible teacher. Talented and dynamic worship leaders from the seminary volunteered their time. Within a year the church was comprised of about two hundred people. Most were young families, many brand new to Christianity. Money was always tight. Half the congregation didn't have any; the other half didn't realize that a church counts on regular tithing to pay the bills. Brandon cut his class load to one-third time with a plan to stretch his last year of seminary into three years.

Things began to get rocky when the photography studio where Brandon worked needed to lay him off. Brandon found a night job at United Parcel Service to help pay the bills. His hours were 4:00 a.m. to 8:00 a.m. When he got off work at UPS, he went home, showered and had breakfast, then went to seminary where he had classes until about noon. From noon until late at night he was involved with running the church. He'd run home, kiss his wife and daughters goodnight, then study for his seminary classes and write his papers until midnight. For three years he kept those hours. Regularly, he slept from just after midnight until his alarm went off at 3:30 a.m., an average of three hours of sleep per night.

By the time Brandon graduated, his marriage was suffering. His health was shot. He hardly recognized his children. His mother-in-law felt put out from picking up the slack in the family. And his church was languishing. Would he do it the same way again?

"Absolutely not," he said.

Brandon now sells insurance. His marriage survived, but his career goal of being an effective long-term church leader did not.

LACKING ONE AREA OF GIFTING

Andrew began his church in all the right ways. He did his homework first. He had denominational backing, which included his salary and the funds for the first two years to rent a building. He planted with a strong and gifted core team. The church quickly grew to about four hundred people. They added children's programs, a youth ministry, an arts ministry, a second Sunday morning service, and then a third service on Saturday nights.

The only problem was that Andrew struggled with his speaking. He never claimed to be a dynamic preacher. He was gifted in vision casting, in gathering a group of people around him, in promoting a church and reaching out to a community. He could manage volunteers and raise funds and create policies and counsel people. He simply couldn't preach.

Andrew brought in an associate who was gifted in preaching. But since it was a church plant, the associate needed to do several other tasks, so Andrew didn't like to have him preach more than once a month. Besides, there were several denominational representatives and older church members who believed that the senior pastor should be the main speaker. So Andrew soldiered on.

He tried hard. He went to conferences and read books and bought tapes and practiced speaking in front of the mirror, but Sunday after Sunday, he struggled with both his nerves and his delivery. After a while, people started to talk. It seemed that when the church first started, a particular group of people noticed Andrew's lack of depth in the pulpit but reassured themselves that a good work was going on nevertheless. They felt called to the church to help with all the new Christians. It was a pioneering work, they told themselves. But the longer they were there, and the longer the preaching continued at the same poor level, this group of people began to feel spiritually hungry, even cheated. They felt angry and frustrated that they weren't getting spiritually fed.

One Sunday morning Andrew vomited before he went on to preach, which wasn't unusual, except that on this morning, he vomited blood. His wife rushed him to the emergency room while the associate pastor took over the morning's services. Andrew had worn a hole in his stomach from all the worrying.

He called the denominational executives and quit the same day.

FOUR HURDLES

What's your story of balance, rest, work, and recharging? If you're like most young church leaders I know, chances are that you haven't got it all figured out just yet. That's okay. It took me a few decades and one physical breakdown before I learned the truth in this area. Maybe you can avoid the breakdown.

Start by asking yourself this: How exhausted are you right now? Take a good, honest look at your life and ask yourself how you feel. If you feel any of the following, know that the warning lights are flashing, and you might not be paying attention to them:

- You are constantly tired and worn out.
- You have stomach pain or some other chronic physical pain or notice you're more angry or irritable than usual.
- You're having a hard time sleeping, or you find yourself more emotional than feels normal.
- Your willpower is low, you have trouble getting up in the morning, you depend on coffee or colas to keep going, or you feel run down all the time.
- Your weight isn't where it should be. You're either overweight or underweight. You eat too much or not enough. You often grab food on the run or not at all.

All of these are signs of mental, spiritual, emotional, or physical exhaustion. Often all four areas of our lives are interrelated. When we become exhausted, we become less adept at our jobs, our relationships and ministry suffer, and our energy levels drop to all-time lows. If we don't do something, exhaustion can lead to consequences such as an increased susceptibility to colds and infections, depression, and burnout.

OUT OF BALANCE
Larry Osborne

What church leaders often don't realize is that constant exhaustion is actually an indication that something is out of balance in life. If we are constantly exhausted, our life-styles are in serious need of examination and change. Long hours, high demands from others, difficult work environments, a constant lack of funding, and other factors can all add up. As leaders, we may not be able to control all of our circumstances, but it is important to take action and combat this condition. We were not meant to function in a constant state of exhaustion.

What does a balanced life look like, one that doesn't lead to constant exhaustion and burnout? It's actually fairly simple. It's when we:

✦ eat right
✦ sleep enough
✦ exercise regularly
✦ spend time with people and hobbies that we love
✦ work appropriate amounts

It sounds pretty simple, I know, but how many church leaders do you know who actually do this?

Throughout his life, Jesus' consistent example is that he ministers, then he gets rest. Often, he walks away from people's needs so he can spend time in prayer and restoration. God's invitation to us, as strange as it may sound, is to do the same. Sometimes a pastor needs to walk away from people's needs. Sometimes he needs to leave people disappointed. Sometimes he needs to say no to opportunities for church or ministerial advancement for the sake of his health. The goal is to never burn out for Christ. The goal is to be consistently usable for kingdom work for however long God has us on earth. We want to be effective today and plan for effectiveness thirty years from now. How can we develop the sustainable ministry habits that will enable us to effectively minister over a whole lifetime? I've found there are four hurdles any minister needs to overcome in order to live a balanced life:

1. *Realize that the work will never be finished.* In pastoral ministry, you are in a peculiar kind of work. A construction worker can point to a series of framed walls at the end of the day. A writer can add up his word count. A project manager can chart a course so he finishes a specific area of development. But a pastor's work is never done. Period. There will always be one more person to help, one more phone call to return, one more message to plan, one more ministry to implement. It also helps to realize that you run your own schedule. Sure, it's okay to have a secretary or administrative assistant help arrange meetings and organize your calendar. But you must establish your own regime. Jesus said you will always have the poor and needy among you (Matt. 26:11). This applies spiritually as well.

2. *Realize that you are not the Messiah.* Jesus is. Your call is not to save the world. That's what Jesus does. Jesus is raising up a lot of other pastors and churches that are just as effective as you and yours. I realized this lesson only after I burned out. For many years, I thought it was all about me and what I could do. Now I know there are a lot of other pastors and churches I need to applaud. I don't need to have the strongest, biggest, or most effective ministry because that's not my value system anymore. I'm not the only pastor on the block, and I'm very happy about that. I need to be praying for other churches and ministries to be raised up and strengthened, and then I need to celebrate them instead of competing with them. One way God gives us rest, strangely enough, is to raise up other people more competent than we are.

3. *Get over self-imposed guilt.* Pastors are prone to feel they can never take a break. There are always so many good and needful things to do. After all, there are so many people who are going to hell without Christ, so how dare we ever sit and fish? How dare we ever take a nap? Perhaps this springs from

noble intentions. But when we truly rest in the sovereignty of God, we recognize that much of our urgency springs from feelings of falsely-imposed guilt, from feelings that if we're not always active we'll be thought of as lazy. This is ultimately harmful to us. God is on the throne. He is in control; we are not. We need to get over our self-imposed guilt and learn to enjoy the gifts God has given to us, to cultivate patterns of recreation and creativity on a constant basis.

4. *Filter others' expectations.* It's easy for people who are not in pastoral ministry to be arm-chair pastors. Everyone's got an opinion about how you should best spend your time. Some of these expectations come from well-intentioned people, those who love us and value our contributions. But we must learn to filter these expectations and learn the fine art of saying no, as well as the skill of delegation. As we talked about earlier, we need to focus predominately on the top 15 percent of activities that *only* we can do.

THE ONE-HOUR EXPERIMENT

Larry, Francis, and I invite you to try an experiment in effective ministry. The best rest we can get is rest that recharges us, that truly provides renewal for our souls. The best rest we can receive ultimately reflects God's call to have a Sabbath, a consistent time that's separate from the work we normally do, a time that reflects God's glory by demonstrating our absolute dependence on Christ.

The experiment is simple. As soon as you finish this chapter and close this book, go do something fun for one hour. That's right.

Fun.

Don't be skeptical. Don't postpone it, and don't insist that you need to get on with the ever-pressing business of church planting. Don't use this time to catch up on the phone calls you need to make, the people you need to visit, the meetings you need to plan for, or the sermon you need to prepare.

Simply take one solid hour and use it to help recharge your soul to the glory of God. If anyone asks, tell them that you're following a prescription mandated by your mentors, Larry, Francis, and

Wayne. We're telling you that you need to do this, because if you're anything like the young church leaders we know, you should have done it yesterday.

Please note that one hour will not be enough. It's just an experiment to test what we are saying. To become a habit that leads to lasting change, it will need to be one hour on a regular basis. The biblical pattern is at least one day off per week. Preferably two.

But just start with one hour to do something completely unrelated to pastoral ministry. Perhaps you could:

◆ Take a walk.
◆ Go to a hobby store you enjoy and browse the newest gear.
◆ Take a nap.
◆ Go for a hike in a nearby park.
◆ Ride a Harley.
◆ Paddle a kayak.
◆ Go horseback riding.
◆ Play with your dog.

Consider this a prescription for ministerial longevity. Go have fun, then take a good look at how you feel afterward. Guilty? Or good? Further behind? Or just a bit recharged for the next bit of God's calling? Know that this one hour of fun is a small sliver of joy that, if you let it, can remind you of heaven. God calls us to enjoy him forever.

Remember that rabbinic saying? "God will one day hold us each accountable for all the things he created for us to enjoy but we refused to do so." So stop refusing. Close the book and begin.

REMEMBER
Develop a sustainable pace.
    Ask yourself, How can I be successful both today and ten years from now?

7

Desperate Times

Reverend Dick Cook, whom everybody called Brother Cook, was a circuit-riding preacher in the eastern part of Oregon during the 1970s. His horse was a maverick, a 1969 Ford Maverick with far too many miles on it. Its rattling muffler hung on by a wire coat hanger that wrapped it to the chassis. His regular Sunday route was an 8:00 a.m. service in Paisley, then an 11:00 a.m. service in Christmas Valley and a 5:00 p.m. in Chiloquin.

I was a Bible college student, an ardent student of homiletics, and ready to take on the world. I had met Brother Cook at a conference, and since I was in the area, I agreed to accompany him on his trail and preach one weekend for him in the three cities. We left early in the morning for Paisley. The road was dotted with Ponderosa pines, and the muffler rattled, signaling that we were on our way. The first tiny country church held about forty-five, and it was packed. I preached my best message, then it was time to greet the congregants who came from farms and ranches spread over the arid countryside. The next stop was Christmas Valley, and there we sat for lunch with the simple farm folk who brought cornbread, chili, and hotdogs. Brother Cook hugged each of the attendees and called each child by name. Then it was off to Chiloquin. The services ended, and I noticed how the people loved this simple preacher who came each weekend to preach and hug.

The two-hour drive home across the evening desert allowed us to converse and visit, but there were also long intervals of silence. I figured I would tap into the elderly veteran for some wisdom, so I posed the mother of all questions: "If you could summarize all that you've learned over many years of ministry, and if you could distill it into one sentence, what one thing would you tell me?"

Not a bad question, right? I waited for the response that would impart to this greenhorn the wisdom of the ages.

He tapped the steering wheel. "One thing?" he asked.

"Yup," I said. "One thing."

He spent the next few minutes lost in thought as I prepared myself for the golden nectar that would fall from his lips and crown my years with goodness. Finally he turned to me and asked, "One thing? Everything I've learned about ministry distilled into one sentence?"

"Yes," I said. "One thing."

"Okay," he said. "Stick with your wife."

Was that all he could come up with? I was shattered. I was waiting for a theological profundity, a Hebrew aphorism that would break the code of all spiritual mystery. But "stick with your wife"? Was that it?

Years have slipped by, and Brother Cook is no longer with us. I've been in ministry for more than three-and-a-half decades, and if I could summarize everything I know about ministry success, longevity, and sustainability, my advice would be the same: "Stick with your wife."

FINISHING WELL

A pastor friend of mine did it right.

His children went off to college, and he was experiencing "empty nest" feelings. It was a bit rough on him and his wife. "All we have is each other now," he reported at a luncheon meeting.

"What are you going to do?" I asked.

"We are going in for marriage counseling," he replied.

Later, I thought how brilliant that was. Why not make the next season the best ever? Why allow unresolved issues, as miniscule as they may be, to be tolerated?

Let me repeat, one day every ministry leader will pack up his desk into a cardboard box, and he will walk out of the office. And when he walks out of the office, he will need to walk into something else. If his family or marriage is shaky, what does he have to walk into?

In the end, when you look back and analyze the effectiveness of your ministry, much of it will come back to you and your spouse. Though I cannot shield you from being sifted in this area, I often hope and pray for church leaders and young planters that their faith will not fail—and that neither will their marriages. In this section, I want to prepare you for the angles that the Adversary will look for to test your marriage so you will be able to recognize them when they come your way. The goal is "that no advantage would be taken of us by Satan, for we are not ignorant of his schemes" (2 Cor. 2:11).

It's most likely that you will be sifted in whatever area you are most vulnerable. You won't be able to take a few online courses or attend a spiritual warfare conference and figure you're set for life. Paul reminds us that we must be on the alert, because our Adversary, the Devil, prowls around like a lion, seeking someone to devour.

WHERE THE ENEMY AIMS

I don't particularly care for dentists, though I guess they aren't really what bother me. It's the sound of the drill that does, so I spend as little time as possible in the dentist's office. While there, I do my best to busy myself with reading or other forms of distraction.

A few weeks back I was at the dentist. There was a stack of magazines on the side table, and I randomly picked up a hunter's journal. The cover depicted a fleeing elk viewed through the scope of a rifle. The crosshairs were aligned on the side of its chest at an angle that, should the shot be taken, the bullet would pierce its heart. I am not a hunter, but I was intrigued by the content of the articles. As I turned the pages, I learned about shooting angles and where the arrow or bullet should enter the prey according to the hunter's position: from above, beside, or diagonally.

The hunter of your soul acts in a similar way. It's as if the Adversary has instructed his minions to determine the best angle at which your heart can be pierced. It won't always be the angle of ministry. It is, more often than not, the angle of your marriage. The Enemy's attacks in this area will pierce your heart and take with it your ministry and influence. And this doesn't necessarily mean that your spouse will be destroyed or that your marriage will fail. It often means that your spouse will live but live wounded.

An old Navy Seal buddy of mine once told me that when in combat, they don't always shoot to kill. Instead, they shoot to wound. When you shoot to kill, you take one person down, but when you shoot to wound, you take at least three out of the battle: the wounded person and two others who have to carry the stretcher. When our spouses live wounded, the enemy not only takes them out, but he often hurts our children as well since they must carry much of the hurt and confusion that results.

FILLING YOUR MARRIAGE TANK

Let me ask you to consider one exercise that may help to save your marriage relationship. It begins with you. In each of us is an emotional reservoir. When we are emotionally filled, we have a sense of well-being and stability. If that tank is drained by excessive tasks or activities that deplete, we feel spent and our patience runs thin. Take some time to picture what you do that fills your emotional reservoir.

Some years ago, I forced myself to sit down with pen and paper and determine exactly which activities replenish my emotional tank and which ones pull the plug and drain me dry. Here is a short list I made of those things that tend to refresh and fill me:

- horses
- riding my motorcycle
- working on our family farm
- traveling
- doing devotions
- music
- dinners with my wife
- golfing
- creatively utilizing the arts for the gospel
- speaking
- training leaders

Equally important, I also duly recorded those activities that drain and deplete me, including:

- excessive paperwork
- unresolved home problems

- working with people who disdain change
- managing instead of leading
- constant deadlines and expectations
- working with staff members who leave unfinished assignments
- supervising those who refuse to take initiative for themselves

Here were the hard facts. The busier I became, the less time I had for what replenished me. For example, I couldn't ride my motorcycle because there were deadlines I had to meet. I couldn't find time to read because I had lessons to prepare. I couldn't get out on the golf course because other more critical demands made golfing seem unimportant. When I did brush the cobwebs off my clubs and carve out a round of golf, I noticed the obvious: my scores accurately reflected my lack of play. Imagine that!

You can tolerate a regimen of more drain than fill for a season, but it will eventually catch up with you. It's like a car that you drive for years without an oil change. You might squeeze twenty or thirty thousand miles out of it, but the neglect will come at the price of an engine that blows a rod or grinds to a stop.

That's the course I was on, and even though the red lights kept flashing on my instrument panel, I couldn't stop. Or maybe it's best to say I *wouldn't* stop. So here is what I did and what I am asking of you:

◀ Write down what fills your tank and what drains it. List at least six things in each category.

Fills	Drains
_____	_____
_____	_____
_____	_____
_____	_____
_____	_____

Now here's the second half. Have your spouse do the same, then share your lists over a nice dinner some evening. Give her the context of what you are doing, then read your lists to one another.

◆ Your spouse's list:

Fills	Drains
_____	_____
_____	_____
_____	_____
_____	_____
_____	_____

Do not comment, argue, contradict, or debate as you read the lists. Just listen, even though your wife may say shopping is what really fills her tank or your husband says golfing every week replenishes him.

Then exchange the lists. You take your spouse's, and he or she takes yours. For the next three months, use that list to guide your prayers for your spouse, promising to help each other by supporting what fills your tanks and doing what you can to alleviate what drains them.

As a husband, I need to know what fills and empties my wife's tank. Pursuing this knowledge has saved my sanity and may have saved my marriage as well.

HOW THIS SAVED OUR MARRIAGE

We moved to Hawaii in 1984 to plant churches, and when we did, we bid adieu to our family and friends in Oregon. Anna's parents lived in Springfield, Oregon, and though we felt terrible about separating our two children from their adoring grandparents, we felt we needed to follow the pillar of fire for our lives. So in a valiant effort to keep her family connected after we moved to Hawaii, Anna called her mother every few days to converse about the children's school activities, the weather, and anything else that came to mind.

After six months of these frequent over-the-ocean chats, I noticed that Ma Bell was taking an increasingly bigger bite out of my wallet. This was in the days when you paid extra for long-distance calling, and as a church planter and novice pastor, there wasn't much in my wallet to begin with. So on one occasion after opening the dreaded monthly billing statement, I announced to my startled wife, "You're talking me right into the poor house! The telephone company stiffed me over $150 this month because of your hour-long conversations with your mother. From now on, if you want to talk to your mother, have her call you. Otherwise, call her collect!" Out of compassion, I later relented, "Feel free to call her once a week, but that's all the mercy I can muster."

My wife has always been so sweet, and she humbly complied. But after a couple of months, I noticed a change in her normally demure disposition. The once shy and reserved princess was slowly mutating into the Wicked Witch of the West. Our relationship turned impersonal and our conversations icy.

I had failed to recognize that talking with her mother was one of the activities that filled Anna's tank. Because she was the only daughter in her family, she was happiest when her relationship with her mom was close and vibrant. They were more like sisters than mother and daughter, and catching up on the latest news about the children was a bright spot in Grandma's week. By cutting Anna off from that connection, I was unwittingly becoming an adversary rather than an advocate. When I realized the imbalance, we made immediate changes. I realized that $150 a month was a very small price to pay for a happy wife. Soon, Anna changed back into the beautiful lady I had married, and springtime returned to the home front. A year and a half later, both her father and mother passed away, and to this day, I dread to think where my marriage would be if I had missed this lesson.

Take the time to do this exercise. It could save you years of sleeping in the doghouse — not to mention saving your ministry. Learn what fills and drains your tank as well as your spouse's. It will help you to restore the fire of friendship. Remember, the key to a success-ful marriage is falling in love again and again, always with the same person.

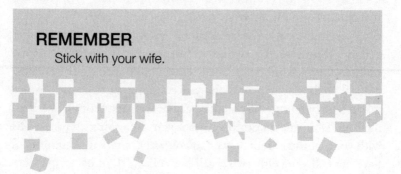

REMEMBER
Stick with your wife.

8

When You Need a Breakthrough

My friend, Gary, once told me a story about his college days, when he ran a quarter-mile relay. It's a very fast race; basically it's just a sprint along the track, and then the baton is handed off to another runner. Each leg of the race takes less than fifteen seconds.

On race day, the grandstands were packed. It was spring and it was a little chilly, so the runners wore sweats over their running shorts until the start of the race. Gary ran anchor, so part of his responsibility was to remove his teammate's starting blocks from the track after the starter's gun went off. Then he was to hightail it back to his box and wait for the baton to hit his hand.

When it was time for the event, the runners staged themselves in their appropriate boxes around the track. Gary positioned himself near the start so he could remove the blocks and then get to his staging box. The gun went off—*bang!*—and the sprint began. Gary dashed to remove the blocks, but one of the foot pegs fell off. He hurriedly scooped up the errant block and hustled over to his starting position with not a moment to lose. He spotted his teammate flying around the curve of the track, all set to hand him the baton. In a flash, Gary remembered he still had his sweatpants on. He whipped them off, positioned himself in his box just in time to feel the baton hit his upraised palm, and he was off like a rocket.

A few steps into his run, he noticed that the day felt colder than it should have. The grandstands were cheering wildly, far more loudly than normal. Glancing down, he suddenly realized that he had taken off more than his sweats. Sprinting toward the finish line and the gathered onlookers, Gary was faced with two options: garner all the courage he could and cross the finish line to the cheers of the crowd or take a sharp left turn across the center field and hightail it to the locker room. Two equally unattractive options.

Continue or quit.

Gary chose the latter.

I rolled with laughter as he told me that story, but his experience reminds me of a more serious dilemma I believe everyone in ministry will face sooner or later. It's a question each ministry leader will eventually ask himself, particularly when the press of being sifted feels suffocating.

Should I continue or quit?

Have you ever faced this question? I have. Quitting is not the worst thing a leader can do. There are times when a fisherman's line gets so tangled he needs to cut his losses for the sake of survival. At other times a leader may decide that God has called him to plant for a comparatively short season, and that season is now complete. Quitting is sometimes the wisest option a leader can choose.

Yet the majority of time, quitting is not the option a leader feels in his heart he wants to choose. The leader really wants to hang on; he's invested so much in the ministry. He's come so far, and he believes he is following God's call. The usual course is to resolve the impingements, rectify the breakdown, and fix the problem. Then, when health is the norm, the leader can revisit his options. If the Spirit of God has him move onward, he can move from a place of health. This is not always the case, but the best changes are the choices we make to follow after the pillar and not to run away from the Egyptians (even though they *are* chasing us!).

THROWING YOUR HEART OVER THE LINE

When I began our pioneering and planting ministry, I was thirty-one years old. My wife and two children and I picked up our lives, left our past, and moved to Hilo, Hawaii. I fell in love with the people and gladly mingled our lives with theirs. It wasn't long before I was convinced that this was where I would spend the rest of my life. I even located a spot on Halai Hill, an aging cemetery, where I'd like to be buried. It was near the remains of one of my ministry heroes, Titus Coan, whom God used to initiate a revival in 1837 that swept the islands.

Ten years passed, however, and God began stirring my heart to pioneer again. We had planted nine other churches when I felt a divine discontent, a soul disturbance that troubled me. I was sure that I was to invest the rest of my life in Hilo, so I was certain that this was only a distraction. My problem was that distraction just wouldn't leave.

The capital of the islands is Honolulu, a city of one million people. Each time I visited it, the city tugged at my heart. After a year of investigating and seeking counsel, I realized that this was more than an interruption. God was involved in this intrusion, and heaven's next step for my life was already in motion. I soon began the process of handing the baton to the next runner and headed across the ocean to Honolulu.

I remember the tug of war I had with God in those days. I had some valid concerns that he needed to address, and at the top of my list was, "If I am to move to another ministry, why did you let me think that this was my last whistle stop? Why did you allow me to believe that I would invest the rest of my life here? Now this move will tear out my heart."

God gently let me know that this was exactly what he intended for me. If I hadn't thrown my heart across the line, if I hadn't lived as if this church were the place where I was investing the rest of my life, we wouldn't have accomplished half of what we were able to achieve. The kind of work that God wanted to do could have been done only by a sold-out heart.

BACK TO FISHING

I believe that how you leave one ministry will determine to a large extent how you will begin the next. But how do you know what your next step is? What do you do if you're caught between the options of staying or quitting, and neither one looks good?

We know that Simon Peter felt this way. Peter is someone I've come to identify with and appreciate over the years. At one time in his life, Peter was a simple fisherman, but then he met Jesus, and Jesus gave him the most inspiring, earth-shattering vision Peter had ever received. Peter would no longer be trolling for bluegill or perch; he'd be fishing for souls. The vision gripped his heart, and Peter left everything and followed Jesus. And Jesus called Peter to simply walk with him — no, not to build a big business, not to become famous, just to walk with him.

Three years passed, and just when it seemed like the ministry was about to take off, Judas got bitter and tainted the whole plan. Jesus was the fall guy. He was betrayed, arrested, and crucified, which put an end to Peter's dreams. Those connected to Jesus were put on the "Jerusalem's Most Wanted" list. Peter himself felt the strain. When confronted and threatened just before his friend, rabbi, and Lord was tortured and crucified, Peter denied even knowing this one who had given him a new direction in life. The painful memory of that night lodged in Peter's heart. Discouragement is contagious, you know, and it wasn't long before the whole team of pioneers chose to call it quits.

The gospel of John reports the story of their decision to quit. Hoping to forget the bad memories, the disciples shoved their boat into the Gennesaret, returning to what they knew best. The first day, out of practice, they came up empty. Evening passed and a new day dawned. In the distance, they spied a lone figure standing on the shore. "Throw your net on the other side of the boat," the voice called. The disciples, with nothing to lose, figured zero from zero would still equal zero. With a shrug, they tossed their net back in. That's when it happened. Not a few, but an abundance of fish suddenly appeared. The nets were jumping with catch as the disciples called in nearby boats for assistance.

When Peter realized that the figure in the distance was indeed Jesus, he jumped out of the boat and swam to shore. Finding the Lord sitting beside a fire roasting fish, Peter sat down and stared. The Lord spoke: "Peter, what have I called you to do?"

Jesus asked Peter the same question he had asked the first time he stumbled upon Peter and his empty nets. There they sat, on the same sandy shore, after three dynamic years of world-changing ministry, and Jesus asked Peter *the* question once again.

The truth we learn here is that whenever you're faced with two options, Jesus shows up. You won't recognize him at first, but hang tight and don't move too quickly until you recognize his voice. Though Peter had already called it quits, Jesus restored him to his original call. And whenever you're about ready to quit, you're going to hear the same thing. The Lord is going to speak to you and ask, "What have I called you to do in the first place?" It may not be the same location, but it will be consistent with your assignment, your one calling. Don't miss that. Relationships may change and geography may shift, but you are still the one he's purchased. We must first remember that we belong to him and his will, not to our own perspective or the path that is most comfortable.

RETURN TO YOUR ORIGINAL CALL

When Peter was ready to quit, Jesus called to him from the lakeside and reminded him of his first call. I believe that's a good example for all of us as leaders. When we feel trapped in a season of sifting and want to quit, we need to return to that original compass. Return to the basics—your first love and your original call.

What was that original call for Peter? Three years earlier, Jesus had spoken to Peter plainly, "Do not fear, from now on you will be catching men," and then Peter "left everything and followed Him" (Luke 5:10–11).

What was your call when Christ first came to you? I'll bet his call wasn't, "Go build a huge megachurch and become famous." Or, "Go take control of your own destiny." And I'd be willing to bet it wasn't, "Go speak fourteen times in two weeks, never see your family, and expend every waking hour serving the needs of other people." I'm going to guess he said something more like this: "Come, follow me. Come, walk with me. Come, find yourself in knowing me."

We so easily forget that this is what's most important in being a leader in the church. Success in ministry must always ratchet us back to that simple truth: it's all about Jesus. It's not "me plus Jesus plus this and that, and then I'll be successful." If that's your plan, then

NEVER LOSE THE AWE AND WONDER
Francis Chan

It's so easy to forget who Jesus Christ really is. As church leaders, we work in a world where prayer, God's Word, and talk about spiritual concepts are all around us. But familiarity has a way of deadening the intensity of a vibrant spiritual life, reducing our wonder and awe at the person of Jesus and what he has done for us. We get caught up in the pragmatic details of running a church and forget why the church actually exists. We forget that we are here to worship God, to serve people in Jesus' name, and to enjoy God forever. Let's never forget the heavenly perspective of this calling.

When I first met my wife, Lisa, I was terrified to speak with her in case I messed up and said something I shouldn't. I remember the very first time I spoke with her on the phone, I actually wrote out notes beforehand about what we might talk about.

Today, after more than seventeen years of marriage, our love is strong and tested, but now when Lisa calls, the conversation is more like, "Hi, what's up?"

Sure, familiarity has dimmed, to some extent, the intensity of our relationship. It happens in any marriage, even if spouses totally love each other, which we do. So our continual invitation to one another is to remind ourselves of the sense of wonder and adoration we first felt for each other at the beginning of our relationship. That's truly what we really feel about each other today, but it's all too easy to forget.

The same can be said for our relationship with God. It's too easy when we pray to simply open our mouths and begin talking. We open or close a meeting in prayer because that's what's expected of us. Instead, we need to be asking, "Who am I about to speak to when I pray?" We need to stop and remember that it's the Lord of the universe, the transfigured Christ.

Keep in mind Hebrews 5:7 (NIV), where Jesus "offered up prayers ... and he was heard because of his reverent submission." That passage really struck me as I was reading it the other day. If Jesus, the eternal Son of God, offered reverent prayers to his Father, my hope is that we, who have been saved by the amazing, undeserved mercy of God, would never lose the sense of awe we should have when we pray or open the Bible.

your identity is fixated on what you can do in your own strength. Eventually, you will taste failure because you aren't following Jesus; you're off doing your own thing.

The sifting process is God's way of bringing us back to our first love and our first call. Though the process is often painful, slowly but surely everything that is unimportant gets cut away. Sifting brings you back to the drawing board, to what is eternal—who you are as a man or woman of God. Sometimes you don't realize that Jesus is all you need until Jesus is all that you've got. In order to bring you to that realization, Jesus will cut everything else out, especially the things you've learned to depend on and trust, so that you will return to him—not to the church or to your identity in ministry, but to who you are in him.

There is only one question that really matters. It's not should I continue or should I quit, it's something else altogether: Is he enough for you?

If you can say yes to that question, you are free to receive what Jesus has for you. When you are rooted in that truth first, your identity won't latch on to the other things that God gives to you, and those other things can't latch on to you and draw you away from your first love.

Have you seen how easy it is for a ministry leader to focus on these secondary things, rather than staying rooted in the love and mercy of Jesus? Many leaders I know have grown comfortable believing the lie that their identity is found in what they do.

◆ When numbers are up, we're happy.
◆ When the church budget is in the black, we're upbeat.

◆ When everybody likes us and nobody is angry with us, we're fine.

◆ If not, we're down.

When you find yourself ready to call it quits, don't be surprised if God removes some of these blessings from your life. He may be tearing you away from the lies you've accepted to bring you back to the truth of his love for you. Always remember that God will provide sufficient grace, and it will often come in times of great weakness. He will give you what you need for the assignment he has called you to do. Grace shields you like an umbrella deflects a downpour and gives you time to figure out what's happening. If you choose to move outside of that covering by responding to circumstances, you'll sense him calling you back, "Come back under the covering. This is where your life can take shape. I will give you the time necessary without the Enemy's intrusion. You are being sifted, and now it's time for you to get your bearings again."

Scripture reminds us that "the name of the LORD is a fortified tower; the righteous run to it and are safe" (Prov. 18:10 NIV). It's okay to be a weak saint when you're in the arms of a strong citadel. Here, in the knowledge of who God is and what he has promised to you, you can recuperate without fear. Let life's intersections be seasons of recalibrating and remembering. Don't simplistically dismiss them as a time of failure or frustration. God does his best work in the desert. As we saw earlier, it's where Moses was called. It's where David developed his skills. It's where John the Baptist carried on his ministry. And it's where Jesus overcame the Devil.

When you are in this season of questioning and searching, asking for direction from the Lord and returning to him, there are three principles that can help you grow and experience greater refinement.

PRINCIPLE 1: LET THE BIBLE STUDY YOU

Jeff Manion wrote a delightful and insightful book called *The Land Between* in which he talks about how we experience these ministry intersections and how hearing God's voice is so crucial. When you need to hear God's voice, circle back to his Word. No, don't approach it as a magical book that will decode your next directive. Instead, look to your time in the Word as a time for reinstilling the most basic discipline of all: a daily devotional time when you sit before God's Word, not in order to study the Bible but to let the Bible study you. Hebrews 4:12 tells us that "the word of God is living and active and sharper than any two-edged sword, and piercing as far as the division of soul and spirit, of both joints and marrow, and able to judge the thoughts and intentions of the heart."

I remember a certain time when I was feeling burnt out and ready to call it quits. I retreated to a mountain monastery to clear my head. Like Elijah coming off Mount Carmel, I was certain that I alone was left to serve him, and I was tired, weary in well-doing. I abandoned everything about ministry for the time being, everything except what I had established years ago, a daily time in God's Word each morning. I needed help and advice, so I turned to my best friends, my mentors in faith, the men and women of the Bible. Every problem you will encounter has already been experienced by someone who has gone before you. These mentors have been designated by God to guide us during times when we feel like giving up.

I was reading Jeremiah in the Old Testament and relating it to my own dilemma and struggle in ministry. I surmised that if there was anyone who understood what I was experiencing, it would have to be the weeping prophet. He had been slandered, thrown into pits, starved, and left for dead. I hadn't gone down that road literally, but it sure felt that way!

The words of Jeremiah 17:16 pierced my heart. I had been grumbling a bit too much, and in an exasperated tone, Jeremiah spoke to me as one friend would to another. It was as if he were sitting there with me, saying, "If you want to leave, go ahead." Then, I felt him turning his face toward heaven, gazing at the Lord, and saying, "But as for me, I have not hurried away from being a shepherd after You" (Jer. 17:16).

Of course, I am adding some color and personal context to the narrative, but I think you get the point. I was running away from my pain, grumbling and nursing my wounds, and without realizing it, I was pulling away—hurrying away, as Jeremiah would say—from God, the one who was best able to mitigate the pain.

The first principle is to press back into God's Word. There is much God will say to you if you are willing to listen, and there is only one book in the universe that God has promised, unfailingly, to speak through.

PRINCIPLE 2: COME TO GOD STUPID

Yes, you read that one right. I could also say it this way: come to him without having the answers already in hand. Turn to God without any presuppositions of the ministry or what you want. Simply say to him, "Lord, I don't know how to be a pastor. I don't know how to shepherd a flock. I don't know how to be a speaker. I don't know how to be a good husband and father in addition to doing everything else I need to do."

I have often come to God as if he were another component I need to add to my stereo system: another amplifier, a sound conditioner, an equalizer, or bigger speakers. I need God to enhance what I am doing and boost my sound quality so my songs sound better. But God doesn't want to boost my songs. He wants to change the music. And unless I come to God stupid, I end up wandering aimlessly down my own path, choosing a secondary route just because I'm too impatient to wait for him in the desert.

God cannot fill a vessel with himself if that vessel is already filled with itself. That's why the Bible says, "blessed are the poor in spirit, for theirs is the kingdom of heaven" (Matt. 5:3 NIV). When you're poor, you have a lot of room in your house. You don't own a thing. Those leaders who are poor in spirit are open to having their hearts cleared from any blame, complaints, or faultfinding. The Lord says, "Just come to me foolish, as you are right now, without the answers. I'll take care of the rest."

PRINCIPLE 3: WRITE IT DOWN!

Then the LORD answered me and said, "Record the vision and inscribe it on tablets, that the one who reads it may run."

—*Habakkuk 2:2*

I cannot overstate this third principle. When you come to listen to God, to meet him in the Word, make sure you come armed with a stack of lined yellow pads or a ream of notebook paper. The best way to solve problems and rethink your next season is to get that inner confusion out of you and onto paper. It's easy to forget what you experience or hear in these moments with the Lord. Writing down your thoughts, impressions, and gleanings from Scripture will be invaluable to you later as you try to summarize and interpret what the Holy Spirit is saying, distilling the most salient points into a clear call to ministry.

I often take notes on what I believe the Holy Spirit is saying to me. I believe this actually honors him when I do it and is dishonoring when I don't. If I am speaking to a young leader and he begins taking notes on what I am saying, I am not dishonored by that. In fact, I am flattered. I tell people that should a young mentee start taking notes when I am talking, I'd make stuff up just so he can continue!

In my ministry intersections, when I face a choice to stay or go, continue or quit, these three principles have held true and helped me to pilot the crosscurrents of ministry storms. They have helped me to navigate through treacherous reefs and brought me to safe harbor. These aren't theories I am suggesting. They don't come from a course I took. These have been learned through navigating stormy seas, through fields of combat and tours of duty.

MOVING FORWARD IN FAITH

I love Peter's response when Jesus begins to correct him, bringing him back to his original call. "Master, we worked hard all night and caught nothing, but I will do as You say and let down the nets" (Luke 5:5). Notice the words "as you say." These words suggest that this wasn't Peter's first choice, that he was tired and ready to quit, but that little phrase made all the difference. Peter came to Jesus and said to him, "at your bidding." In other words, "Lord, I will do it. If this is what you want, it's what I'll do. I will move forward in faith. If you say so, consider it done."

In any season of sifting, there will be times when you don't feel like doing something, but because God asks you to, you do it anyway.

At these times when everything in you says, "No way," yet the Lord directs you and says, "Move forward in faith," your response must be, "Lord, at your bidding, I will go." This is the response of a surrendered disciple, one who has been stripped of everything but the desire to serve and follow his Master and Lord. If we're honest, we may want to revisit some of the things that came up empty the first time, such as that church plant that never took root and flourished. But again and again, the Lord turns us back and says, "Yes, your net came up empty the first time, but if you let down the nets again *at my bidding*, not because you're expecting results the way you imagine them, then you'll find the catch." And when you revisit your call with this new motivation, you'll indeed find a catch.

Peter must have caught onto this truth as he stirred the embers that second time around the fire on the beach. Jesus had prepared breakfast for the disciples. They'd eaten their fill of bread and fish, and then Jesus took Peter for a little walk, all by himself.

"Simon son of John, do you love me more than these?" Jesus asked Peter (John 21:15 NIV). He never asked Peter about his failures; he didn't ask about his denial. Jesus never brought up the past. He just focused on Peter's heart. What did he love? "Do you love me more than these?" Jesus asked. "Do you love me more than your old way of life?" He wasn't just talking about fish but about all the desires Peter had allowed to cloud his assignment: "Do you love me more than a good reputation? Do you love me more than having money? Do you love me more than having everyone like you? More than losing face or being successful in business? If everything were gone except your relationship with me, would that still be enough for you?"

Peter thought for a moment then said, "Yes, Lord, I do." I don't think it was a hard decision for Peter, not when he thought it through. There Jesus was, the Creator of the universe, the Author of life, the one who brings all success and purpose and security and significance into the world, the one who, with a word, created light, and he was asking Peter if he was enough?

"Then feed my sheep," Jesus said. "Go back to what I asked you to do in the first place." In other words, "Come follow me." With that Peter found his way home again. At Jesus' bidding.

WHEN YOU LONG FOR BREAKTHROUGH

There are times in your life as a leader when, like Peter, you want to quit. The season of sifting you're in feels too difficult. You've been desperately striving for breakthrough, but it hasn't come. What do you do now?

Sometimes, the work of God is to strip us of our identity, even if that means quitting a particular ministry that we've been doing. Sometimes, the ministry is taken from us. Either way, there is no shame in leaving behind a role we've felt called to for a season if God wants us to quit or if a door closes due to circumstances. In fact, this can be part of the refining process. But to quit being a minister altogether or to quit a particular ministry for the wrong reasons—to feel relief, or to be in control, or to run to anything other than your call—will never be God's best for your life.

My encouragement, in the midst of this season of sifting, is to hand over your life with reckless abandon and entrust your future to Jesus. Don't call it quits for the wrong reasons. And don't try to push through and make it on your own, returning to the empty fishing nets. Surrender to him, and he will bring about the breakthrough he wants for you, in his time and way.

That breakthrough may take the form of Jesus leading you to a new geographical place or a new ministry. It may take the form of Jesus leading you within the sphere of your present ministry to a new experience of victory. As you surrender to him, he will do the leading. He'll lead you to a place of abundance in ministry in the midst of a land of emptiness.

And when, once again, your nets are overflowing with fish, he will invite you to share a meal with him on the shore and remind you why you do it all in the first place.

REMEMBER

Ministry intersections are not endings; they hold new beginnings.

PART THREE

hard
work

Hard: *adjective*
Complex or troublesome with respect to an
action, situation, or person.
Involving a great deal of effort, energy, or
persistence.
    Difficult to deal with, manage, control,
overcome, or understand.

A sifted life is an influential life. Your greatest influence takes
place after you have been sifted and have survived. Who is the
person who has the most credibility when someone is diagnosed with
cancer? It's the woman who has wrestled with cancer and survived.
Who is the man who can speak with authority and persuasion to the
inmates at the jail? It's the one who has been behind bars himself and
has returned to reach those still on the inside. Unsifted Christians
won't have as much influence, and that's simply the way God has
designed it to be. Sifting is how God separates the old from the new,
the good fruit from the bad, the material that is unusable from that
which God can effectively employ for his eternal purposes.

My son, Aaron, had recently graduated from Bible college, and
we were sitting down at a local coffee shop for early morning devotions, one discipline that we sometimes share together. With a smile
on his face, he said to me, "Well, Dad. I'm done! Hallelujah!" I
clapped and hoorayed with him. He cheerfully continued, "I guess
I'm now ready for ministry!"

"Well," I said, raising my eyes to look at him. "Not quite."

"But Dad, I graduated! I'm done!"

"Yes," I said. "But you still lack one thing. One thing that will
make you ready to be used by God."

"I've taken the classes, I've studied, I've worked. What could that be?" he asked, a bit confused.

"Son, you haven't suffered enough yet."

Sifted saints uniquely understand the pain, the suffering, and the plight of life in a fallen, broken world. Suffering ratifies your ministry. It's not something you volunteer for, and you don't have to sign up for it. You don't even have to look for it.

If you are faithfully following God, it will find you.

First Peter 4:12 reminds us of a powerful truth that we easily forget: "Beloved, do not be surprised at the fiery ordeal among you, which comes upon you for your testing, as though some strange thing were happening to you." Peter encourages us not to be surprised, not to think that suffering is something strange or unusual in the Christian life. Sifting is normal, the natural result of following Jesus and serving God in a broken world. It's something we should expect and something we should prepare for. We must be ready to persevere, to push through the difficult seasons, working with all our strength while depending on the grace of God to sustain us. In this book's final section, we'll examine the third part to ministry success in difficult seasons. It isn't the most popular, but it is one of the most important factors: hard work.

Hard work is not at odds with rest and balance. Taking time to rest implies that you are already working, and hard work is the mark of a committed servant. The work we're referring to here is not the senseless activity of the workaholic, feeding an addiction. I know firsthand the pain of burning out and relying on my own wisdom and strength in all the wrong ways. Instead, I encourage a biblical emphasis on loving God with all of your heart, soul, mind, and strength—giving the best of your energy, time, and effort to serving the Lord.

The Bible tells us that we are to work six days, and on the seventh day, we are to rest. But sometimes, in our attempts to strike a balance, we mix these up. Hard work is definitely an integral part of the ministry equation, though it must necessarily be balanced by appropriate times of rest and refreshment. The Bible is filled with examples of godly men who pushed themselves to the limit, giving all they had to serve the purposes of God. I am captured by the heart of Gideon in Judges 8:4, where we read that he was "weary yet pursuing"; though exhausted, Gideon persevered and won the day. What a great picture of single-minded devotion! Or consider Eleazar, one of David's thirty mighty men in 2 Samuel 23, who fought the Philistines until his hand was weary, yet he still clung to the sword. The Bible tells us that "the LORD brought about a great victory that day" (2 Sam. 23:10).

Much of ministry is simply hard work, pure sweat equity, hand-to-the-plow, daily-grind effort. Sometimes this means slogging through a difficult season in which every day it is a chore to get up and out of bed. Sometimes this means traversing seasons of intensity: walking with your people through a suicide in your church or a community tragedy. Often, you will suffer alongside the people you serve, and there will be long days of hurt and pain.

In the information age in which we live, technology has a way of selling us on convenience. If something can't be done electronically, we are not interested in doing it. But the bottom line for effective ministry must never be our own convenience. It takes blisters, commitment, and a willingness to go wherever the Lord leads us to get it done. This may be a foreign concept to some leaders; I find that many aspiring leaders operate under the myth that there is an effective methodology or a ministry secret that can replace hard work and perseverance. Instead of hard work, they believe that somewhere there's an app for their problem that will make everything simple and easy. There is no easy road to success in church leadership. If I could repeat this line to you one hundred times, I would.

Over the next four chapters, we'll take a look at how to cultivate the character needed to work hard and prepare for a season of sifting. One of the most difficult things for a leader to develop is a bias for action. Without it, you'll never develop a forward lean to your ministry, and without it, you'll never have fresh vision. This is another way of saying that whatever comes your way, you won't shrink back and retreat. You'll be committed to living courageously and decisively, and you'll be committed to undertaking difficult tasks. But how do you develop this bias? How do you cultivate courage and boldness to continue leading during times of difficulty and trial in your ministry?

9

Hand to the Plow

A few months back, I spoke at a youth pastors' conference. In a small group forum, one young leader complained that he didn't have much time for anything anymore.

"Why, just yesterday," he said, "I had 136 emails to answer, and after I went through them my Facebook needed updating. Then I wrote on my blog, updated Twitter, and did some research on Wikipedia. Before I knew it, it was 5:00 p.m. The next day, I had to answer just as many emails, but then I had three magazines on youth ministry I had to read through, my Facebook account to check, and I took two of my youth group students to watch midnight movies. It's been like this for the past five days! I'm pooped!"

I had to contain myself. Certainly, relationship building is part of the ministry process, and online interactions constitute a big piece of youth culture these days. But the truth is that today it is far too easy to substitute busywork for the real work of ministry. We can send and receive hundreds of emails, check our Facebook feeds constantly, tweet till the birds go deaf, and watch dozens of the best new movies to be up on culture, but in the end no one gets saved, no one is invited into a deeper relationship with Jesus, no one is challenged to go into ministry, and no new spiritual leaders are raised up. We rationalize our activities as opportunities for relationship building, but far too often, we fail to cross those bridges and bring an invitation to discipleship where people hear Jesus say, "Come, follow me."

To be clear: church leadership is not about filling our days with a flurry of office activity. It's about taking strategic steps to present the gospel and guide people to spiritual maturity. After listening to this youth pastor, I pressed him a bit further and asked him how he thought he might become more effective in his work. I hoped that he would talk about strategies to lead students into a closer relationship with Christ and invite them to a greater depth of spiritual leadership. But sadly, I heard none of that. Instead, without hesitating, he said to me, "What we really need is some better software to develop a database for our kids, and I think I might need to hire an assistant to help me. I've asked my pastor if I could hire someone, but he said the church didn't have the budget."

I wanted to say it, but I didn't: "Why don't you just turn off your computer and *get to work?*"

I believe that many church leaders have developed some unbiblical work habits, mistaking busywork for the real work of ministry.

- We place too much emphasis on spiritual gifts and too little on sweat and gumption.
- We affirm God's omnipotence but focus little on our own obedience.
- We talk about God's attributes and his work but fail to act in response.
- We place too much emphasis on technology and information and too little on God's presence and incarnation.

If you're going through a season of sifting right now, you may need to ask yourself a tough question: Were you ever prepared for how much hard work it would take? Were you ready to sacrifice, to give what is required to be a fruitful servant of the Lord? The real work of church ministry is not holing up in an office somewhere. It's about developing a bias for action.

As a grandfather, I've noticed that I can sometimes mess up my grandkids by the way I tend to express my love. Yes, that's right, I mess them up. I tell them, "I had to walk three miles each way to school every day, and both ways were uphill." They laugh and roll their eyes at my exaggeration, but it's partly the truth — the three miles that is. I attended a small Bible college, and we walked each day in wind, rain, and fire. (Okay, that last part is not true.)

But because I remember the struggles and hard work, I find myself trying to protect my grandkids from what I experienced. And that's where I mess up. My attempt to spare them the hardships I endured as a young man is an unhealthy way of expressing love. Still, it's a common response of many parents and grandparents, particularly in the Boomer generation. We drive our kids and grandkids to private schools. We arrive early to pick them up because Lord forbid if we are late.

We succeeded in building a soft generation who have been told repeatedly how wonderful they are, who have never experienced what it means to sweat, develop blisters, and put in long hours without overtime pay. Many have been raised in schools that believe it is wrong to give failing grades and hesitate to mark anyone down for mistakes. Many kids today have never been cut from a team because everyone plays, and no matter how bad you are, everybody gets a trophy. This sounds gracious, but it breeds a generational addiction to affirmation that can easily lead to an aversion to correction and reproof. Being told that they don't measure up, that they have failed, or that their work does not meet the acceptable standard can be a crushing blow to the next generation of leaders.

In ministry, this easily translates into a sense of entitlement, the sense that ministry is primarily about finding something worthwhile and fulfilling, a rewarding experience that meets our desires. Even when we talk about serving others, we emphasize that the goal of serving is feeling good about yourself. We've turned serving into something of privilege, a benefit with rewards.

I won't deny the truth that there are blessings to be found in serving Jesus, and they are wonderful and good. But fundamentally, being a servant means serving others. It's not about getting what you want or pleasing yourself. Servants often must forsake their own needs, wants, and desires for the good of their master. And while every Christian wants to be known as a humble servant, especially in leadership circles, the truth is that nobody wants to be treated like one. The true test of a servant is how you respond when you are treated like one.

DO YOU DO WINDOWS?

Whenever he hires new church staff, a good friend of mine will always ask at some point in the interview, "But do you do windows?" He is not asking if they are savvy with the Microsoft operating system; he literally means washing windows. It doesn't matter to him if the person he is hiring is a talented worship leader, staff counselor, or computer expert. He wants to know if they have the servant-heartedness to do whatever it takes to get the job done.

All of our church planters first train as apprentices or interns within our ministry, some for five years and others less, before we allow them to plant a church. I still remember when some of our current pastors first came to us to prepare for ministry. Some came as corporate executives, some as students, and one even came as a former circuit court judge. Regardless of their background, they all started with the same initial responsibility in the program: latrine duty.

No joke.

Some did this for a year, some longer. It all depended on their ability to scrub porcelain. My son, Aaron, who just turned thirty-one, is today pastor of an eight-hundred-member church about twenty minutes east of the mother campus. While in Bible college, his summer internship was latrine duty. He did this for two years, and at the beginning of his third summer, I called him into my office to congratulate him. I was going to promote him. He was excited and expectant. "What do I get to do this summer?" he asked. I replied, "You have done so well, this summer I am promoting you to oversee the other latrine scrubbers. Congratulations!" As you might expect, that didn't thrill him as much as it did me, but he accepted his new post. For the next two years until he graduated, he excelled in bathroom basics. I told him that when he graduated from Bible college, I would award him the "super bowl" trophy.

I am so proud of our church planters, and the ones who seem to do the best are the ones who start with the least. It's where all servants start.

THE GREATEST ARE SERVANTS

As a leader in the church, one of the areas in which you will be sifted is your willingness to be a servant. Consider what Jesus teaches his disciples in Luke 22:26–27: "The one who is the greatest among you must become like the youngest, and the leader like the servant. For who is greater, the one who reclines at the table or the one who serves? Is it not the one who reclines at the table? But I am among you as the one who serves." Looking for Jesus? Check the servants' quarters.

Luke tells us that the greatest can qualify for the work of ministry only as servants. In the business world, you start off as a page boy and you distance yourself from that role as soon as you can. But in the kingdom, you graduate to servanthood. In the kingdom, only the greatest can be servants. Why? Servants must be great in patience. Servants are great in forgiveness, endurance, consistency, faithfulness, dependability, and trustworthiness. Each of these virtues is earned and developed through trial and testing. They aren't simply granted to you because you study about them or read about them. You get them by being sifted, and if you drop out of the sifting process, you will never gain the experiences necessary to go the distance. As Jesus said to Peter before his testing: "I have prayed for you, that your faith may not fail; and you, when once you have turned again, strengthen your brothers" (Luke 22:32). God's testing refines us in our failure, helping us to develop a deeper grasp of what it means to serve as we ourselves are served by God's gracious love and forgiveness. And unless we understand the importance of true servanthood, our people will have a very difficult time seeing Jesus in our churches. The truth is that people don't need to see you or me as the person with all the answers. They don't need our multimedia presentations or our nice campus. They simply need to see Jesus. And here in Luke 22, Jesus reminds us where he will be found. He is among us as one who serves.

Some years ago, a sour looking man came to one of our New Hope services and found himself a conspicuous spot on the front row. He crossed his arms and glued them there for the whole service. Seeing his demeanor, and enjoying challenges, I set myself to winning him over. But my best anecdotes fell flat, and my finest illustrations went unnoticed. At the end of the message, I gave people an opportunity to receive Christ. I usually ask people to close their eyes and bow their heads, but he remained rigid, eyes wide open, and arms still folded. The service concluded, and I breathed with relief as he got in his car and left.

The following week, however, he returned. Same seat. Same posture. Same response.

Then the next weekend arrived, and so did he, like a recurring migraine. I gave the best of my humor, uncorked my top illustrations, and really pulled out the dog and pony show. I called on the Father, Son, and Holy Ghost to somehow minister to this naysayer, but the results were the same. No change. No response. No nothing.

After the last service, as I was visiting with some congregants, this man came to me and asked if he could have a word. I consented, and we walked off to the side. He said, "I have made a decision to make this my home church." I stood frozen, a bittersweet moment of ambivalence and fear. "Wonderful," I managed to say without inflection. "I am happy for you."

"Oh, it's not because of you," he said.

"Great," I managed to say. "That inspires me."

"Do you want to know why?" he said to me. "It's because of the servants here. You see, I came three weeks ago because I heard about this church. I didn't believe anything people told me. So I came to check it out myself. And at first, I thought you had a plastic smile. No one can be that happy. So I came the second week to see if it was still there. Then I figured the third week, I'd check out the people. I was talking with some of the volunteers here, and when I turned to leave, I slipped. I missed the curb and stumbled toward a stone wall. I couldn't catch myself, but one of the young men dove to catch me, sacrificing himself as I fell on him instead of the stone wall. He tore his shirt but was concerned only with my welfare and not with any of his injuries. He said it was such a blessing for him to see that I was uninjured! It was at that point that I knew this church was the real thing. That's why I am making it my home church."

Jesus is always found among those who serve. If there are no servants and we're just performers, people will be hard pressed to see the one who serves by saving and redeeming them. They will see videos that describe him, hear messages that espouse him, but without sacrificial service, the real Jesus will be hard to spot. Once when many of our church leaders were gathered I asked them, "How many greeters do we have here?" Twenty people raised their hands. I then asked, "How many ushers?" Thirty lifted theirs. I continued, "How many custodial workers do we have in the room?" A dozen identified themselves.

I paused and said, "What if we all greeted? We all can greet people, can't we? And what if we all ushered? If someone needs help, any one of us could do that, couldn't we? And what if we all cleaned up? If there's a stray piece of paper, I bet I could pick it up without having to go through an orientation class that trains paper picker-uppers! Let's all be greeters, ushers, and cleaners. How's that? Here's the reason: if Jesus is seen among servants, and only a few are serving, people are hard pressed to see Jesus when they come to New Hope. But if we all enlist as servants, when people show up, they'll see Jesus everywhere! So, on my next question, let's all raise our hands."

"How many servants do we have in the room?" Everyone raised their hands, applauding as they realized that Jesus is seen when we serve.

WHATEVER IT TAKES

If cleaning windows or latrines is beneath a minister or church leader, he or she will eventually come to a quitting point. When I began, it didn't matter to me if I had a degree, letters of recommendation, or letters behind my name. I simply said, "Whatever it takes."

Many church planters go from a relatively stable job that includes regular pay to an entrepreneurial, risk-taking endeavor with an uncertain future. Fundraising is a new challenge, and many planters begin with little or no training. I remember my first experience in ministry, working with Youth for Christ. It was a challenging and exciting time of seeing the Lord work, and I enjoyed the season immensely, but one thing that was challenging for me was raising my own support. I can't say I enjoyed that part of the job. I knew nothing about raising support and made plenty of mistakes along the way, but that experience taught me how to generate financial backing, how to be thrifty with funds, and how to see each dollar as a gift. A few years later, after I graduated from Bible college, I began a new position as a youth pastor, teaching pastor, and worship leader. That position was salaried. If anything, my experience with Youth for Christ taught me to be thankful for this new salaried position. I knew never to take a paycheck for granted because I knew firsthand how much work it took to generate one.

After a successful season of serving in that salaried staff position, I moved to Hawaii to plant a church. And guess what? I had to raise my support all over again. All that the backing church could afford to give me was a housing allowance. Everything else, I had to raise. Thankfully, this time around, I knew what I was doing.

By 1995, our church plant was flourishing. The church had grown to two thousand people, and I was no longer a bivocational pastor. Everything looked smooth. We had just finished construction of our church building on the twenty acres of land we'd purchased, and I thought everything was set for the future. But then the Lord said, "Start all over again."

We traveled to Honolulu, 250 miles north, to plant yet another church, New Hope Oahu. And yet again I had to raise support until the church took off. For the first year, the church couldn't pay me a salary. I raised my own support, knowing that I had three children at home and bills that needed paying. Some funding came from our former ministry, and for the rest, I relied on money generated from speaking and writing to help make ends meet. After a year, I felt that the first person we should salary was an administrator, so I waited another six months before accepting a salary from the church. When it finally happened, I was thrilled. But then, when I received my first check, I sensed the Lord asking something of me. I felt that he wanted me to give this first paycheck back to him as a burnt offering, so I turned it over, signed my name, and dropped it in the offering plate. It wasn't an easy thing to do, but it was healthy for my soul, freeing me of the temptation to depend on my salary and not on the Lord.

I was being sifted, but it was good for me. Tough, but good. I learned to trust God.

There's a powerful truth in Isaiah 48:10: "Behold, I have refined you, but not as silver; I have tested you in the furnace of affliction."

EXERCISE WISDOM WITH FINANCES
Larry Osborne

Research shows that the average church plant takes three or more years to become financially self-sufficient. During that time, church planters often need to rely on financial support from other churches and donors. Church planters report that the journey to becoming financially self-sufficient often places a heavy burden on the church planting family. One of the most common — and impacting — financial pitfalls of church planting comes when planters drain their savings and retirement accounts to pursue their dreams. This can be a catalyst for stress in a marriage and family.

Exercise godly wisdom and discernment, and be prepared for things to take longer than you expect. Don't rush to drain your finances for the sake of the church. God may be using this time to train and teach your people, calling them to greater involvement and sacrifice as they make financial investments in the future of the church. If God said to drain it, fine. But if we drain it, and then say, "God, fix it for me," it's not so fine.

Any of these money situations could have derailed me from God's calling. When I first began in pastoral ministry, I wrestled with the time it took to raise support. I could have easily called it quits. When I left my salaried position to begin a church plant that required me to raise support again, I could have refused and stayed where I was, secure and comfortable. And when I left yet another stable church to plant another, I could have been bitter and resentful of having to raise support yet again. But where would all of that have gotten me? The Lord knew my future, so he brought me along a pathway where I was able to learn the necessary skills. Over time, I began to look upon these seasons of fundraising and working bivocationally as a time of teaching. I saw my past as a mentor, and I refused to grow embittered by those life experiences. Instead, I trusted that God was at work and that he knew what he was doing. I knew that he needed to teach me something, and yielding to him would bear fruit for the future.

WHAT WE PRACTICE FOR

Some years ago, I prepared for one of the most grueling water races in the ocean around Hawaii. It's a forty-one-mile canoe race across a treacherous channel between the islands of Molokai and Oahu called the Ka'iwi channel. The currents run swift, and the waves can be over eight feet high, sometimes pushing boats into the cliffs on the east shore of the island. My training regimen began eight months before the race. I ran, lifted weights, dieted, and paddled for hours. My endurance increased, and I worked on improving my ability to weather fatigue. Several times I ran for three to four hours in the noonday sun to build my stamina. I wanted to persevere and finish the race.

Finally the day of the race arrived. At 6:30 a.m., more than one hundred canoes were at the starting line, and a green flag signaled the start. Paddles hit the water with force, and the five-hour event was under way. The racers were focused, sprinting ahead, as escort boats paced us along the way. The first hour we ran on pure adrenaline. By the second hour, we had to dig a bit deeper. By the third hour, the sun began taking its toll, and several paddlers dropped behind in exhaustion. By the fourth hour, dehydration set in for some, and the line of canoes started thinning out. At that point, I started to wonder why I had ever signed up for this tiring race. Everything in me began shutting down, one muscle group at a time. I struggled to breathe in the heat of the sun, and everything was intensified by the glare off the ocean. My arms and back cramped. I found that I couldn't distinguish between hallucination and reality, and I honestly thought I saw a couple of mermaids swim by. They were most likely tiger sharks, but nevertheless, they looked like they were having a whole lot more fun than I was.

Just as I reached the point of giving up, abandoning ship and calling for the escort boat, a clear thought came to me: "*This* is what I have been training for! Not just for the race—it has all been for *this moment* in the race!" This is what all the dieting had been for, all the weights and the marathons in the heat of the day. All of my training was for this precise moment. I hadn't trained for the first hour. I had plenty of energy then. And my training wasn't for the end of the race. I knew there would be plenty of well-wishers there to encourage me. No, it was for this very moment when no one else was around. I had trained to push through the time when there is no one cheering, when everything inside of me is telling me to quit.

This is exactly what I had been practicing for!

No one practices for a vacation. You don't need to prepare for something like that. You don't need to prepare for an afternoon nap. No, you prepare for that point in the race when you are depleted and fatigue has beaten you down. You prepare for the moment when you want to quit, when you are tempted to be unfaithful to your wife or stomp out of a board meeting in anger. These moments are why we listen to hundreds of sermons, read dozens of books, and wade through mountains of articles. We do it all so we won't quit.

I realized, in that moment, that if I dropped out of the canoe race in the final hour, it would nullify the hundreds of hours I had put into preparing. Suddenly, it was like nitric oxide had been added to my tank. I felt refreshed and invigorated, and I dug that paddle in deep with a new lease on life. It was my best race ever.

YOUR PAST IS A MENTOR FOR YOUR FUTURE

Your past holds dozens of these events, defining moments where your faith fails or builds, faith that God knows we will need for what lies ahead in the years to come. Our Father knows the end from the beginning, and he allows sifting to take place because he knows precisely what we will need for the circumstances of tomorrow in our marriages and in our ministries. Specific faith is built in specific instances. When David was a young boy, he killed a lion and a bear. At the time, he could not have known that he would one day face Goliath, who taunted the armies of the living God. Yet the hardships of his past taught him to rely on God in the challenges he faced later. Or consider Caleb, who in Joshua 14 celebrated his eighty-fifth birthday by launching a successful attack on the sons of Anak and was given the city of Hebron. The kind of faith that leads an eighty-five-year-old man to courageously enter the fight again was developed forty-five years earlier when he and eleven others spied out the Promised Land; along with Joshua, Caleb's faith in God grew and was refined through that experience, even though at the time he was in the minority.

Because God is faithfully working through the circumstances of our lives for our good and for his glory, you can trust that the experiences of your past can be used by God to prepare you for what you will face in the future. If you dismiss difficult events or grow bitter, envious of what others have and you do not, you will miss the lesson of sifting, and with it the development of the faith you will need for the season you are about to face.

My dad was a first sergeant in the army. He was a highly disciplined man, and he parented from a military perspective. He laid down the stripes until I saw the stars! I can't say I enjoyed his parenting techniques at the time. When I was a boy, my family traveled from base to base, never having roots in one location for more than three years at a time. I was still young when my parents divorced and a bitter custody battle ensued. Within a few years, my father remarried, and one of my brothers and I moved to Oregon with our new family.

During my first year of high school, I attended a private Catholic school in California. My mother passed away that year, and my life took a wrong turn. I began using drugs and was later expelled for stealing. My relationship with my father grew worse, and I dropped out of school in the middle of my senior year. I moved 250 miles north to Portland, Oregon, where I joined a rock group and made my living playing shrill guitars through ear-piercing amplifiers.

Eventually, I completed my high school requirements and enrolled in a junior college where Campus Crusade had an active program, and through the invitation of a girl on the ministry staff, I opened my heart to Christ, entered Bible college, and later began to serve in ministry with Youth for Christ. My past was far from ideal, and even after I became a Christian, I struggled for many years to overcome some fairly serious character malformations.

But here is the honest truth: if I had to do it all over again, I wouldn't change a thing. I believe that even when I was a young boy, God knew what my future calling would require of me, and in his all-encompassing wisdom and grace, he placed me in an environment that would develop the necessary quick twitch muscles that would keep me in the race. I learned discipline from being the son of a tough first sergeant. Being raised in a broken family, I quickly learned to fend for myself. When you are a pastor, Sunday follows Sunday follows Sunday, and it demands a consistent discipline each week to prepare messages along with the other myriad responsibilities of any growing ministry. Many of the disciplines that I rely on today were formed in my childhood years of learning to do whatever it took to survive difficult times.

My encouragement to you is to not disparage your past. You can choose to make it your teacher, or it will become your torturer. You can assign to your past experiences whatever role you choose, but choose wisely how you interpret and process them. Depending on how you understand and respond to your past, it can make you better, or it can embitter you. You can live in regret over your past, or you can allow the gracious love of God to bring you confidence for your future.

Learn from your history, because it is connected to your future. Remember these three scriptural principles that will help to make your past a mentor.

> The Lord has allowed you to go through everything you have been through, both positive and negative, for a reason (Rom. 8:28).
> You might never know or understand the reasons why you went through some things. But be assured that God, who began a good work in you, will complete it (Phil. 1:6).
> Nothing touches your life unless it has gone past God's desk. He has allowed it because he knows it will build you for what lies ahead (1 Peter 2:9).

Take some time to think through your past and answer the following questions, either on paper or with the help of a trusted friend.

◢ The thing, event, circumstance, or person that affected me most in the past and still tends to affect me most in my present role is:

_____

_____

_____

_____

◢ It tends to affect me in this way:

_____

_____

_____

_____

◢ If I imagine my past as a mentor, this is what I believe my past should teach me:

_____

_____

_____

_____

REMEMBER

Make your past a mentor and you will be granted the faith God knows you will need for the future.

10

Assessing Character

The year was 1970; I was a senior in high school, and I thought I was quite a runner. I remember one particular cross-country race we ran against an obscure high school called Marshfield High in southern Oregon. One of my competitors that day was a kid named Steve. When the gun went off at the start of the three-and-a-half-mile race, this kid took off as if he had been stung by hornets. I laughed to myself, thinking, "Look at that crazy man. We'll find him passed out at the two-mile marker, I'm sure. And when I do, I'll just step over him with a smile." Well, at the two-mile marker, he wasn't there. In fact, I didn't meet up with him the entire race. When I finally crossed the finish line, he had already donned his sweats and was sitting on a lawn chair sipping lemonade. What I didn't know back then was that the Steve I was running against was none other than Steve Prefontaine.

After that race, I realized that I wasn't quite the runner I had thought I was. I had been a legend in my own mind, but that was about it. Steve, on the other hand, would actually go on to become a legend. In his junior year of high school, Prefontaine went undefeated and won the state title. In his senior year, he had another undefeated season, set a national record at the Corvallis Invitational, and won two more state titles—one in the mile and the other in the two mile. He went on to the University of Oregon, where he won every meet he entered. He won the NCAA Men's Cross Country Championships three of his four years at Oregon, sitting out in 1972 to train for the Olympics. At one time in his career, Prefontaine held the American record in seven distance track events from the 2,000 meter race to the 10,000 meter race. He is considered by many to be one of the most gifted runners of all time.

While Steve was at the University of Oregon, Bill Bowerman, his running coach, was experimenting in his garage with some new shoe designs. He made his first sets of custom running shoes using rubber soles he had vulcanized on his wife's waffle iron. Steve ran with these shoes, but they found that the adhesive lasted for only one race. Bowerman turned to entrepreneur Phil Knight, and together they worked on perfecting the running shoe. Today, the company they founded, Nike, is the world leader in athletic shoes and apparel.

But Steve Prefontaine didn't live to enjoy his success. In 1975, returning from a party, he was speeding around a park in Eugene, Oregon, when his orange MGB convertible flipped, pinning him beneath the chassis. Tragically, he couldn't free himself and died of suffocation at the young age of twenty-four.

Why do I share this story? There are two lessons I find in the story of Steve Prefontaine. The first is a reminder to me that even though I thought I was strong, I was really just deluded. My self-assessment fell far short of reality. And that's a lesson for all of us. As leaders, doing an honest self-assessment gets complicated. How do we accurately assess our skills, talents, gifting, or character?

The second lesson, perhaps even more profound, is that Steve Prefontaine was an incredibly gifted man who had success on the track and who would have undoubtedly found success in the business world, but all of that success was cut short in an instant. The truth is that success, whether it results from our skills, talents, gifting, or character, is always fragile. If we assume that we are the reason for our success, we are fools.

These two lessons lead me to the questions I want to examine in this chapter: What does it mean to truly assess yourself, to look at who you are at the core? And how does that assessment relate to your success?

UNGUARDED STRENGTH

Abraham Lincoln was a dedicated Christian. He was also a convincing orator. Before he approached a platform to speak, he prayed, but it was not what you or I might pray. Instead of praying, "God, without you, I will fail," he'd courageously pray, "God, without you, I must fail." Lincoln knew that he could sway the people, but it might not be in a God-honoring way. He was profoundly aware that his great gift could be his greatest weakness, and he knew that without God he was guaranteed to fail, even if the speech was well liked and applauded.

Assessing ourselves is necessary because we are often blind to our greatest weaknesses. Why? Because it is our unguarded strengths that become our greatest weaknesses. It is incredibly difficult to see the things you are good at as a potential liability. Undoubtedly, you will readily recognize the following names: John Dillinger, Al Capone, Lucky Luciano, Benito Mussolini, Adolf Hitler, Osama bin Laden. What do they all have in common? They were all, at one time in their lives, gifted leaders with great potential. They all had brilliant minds and were influencers of others. But all of them squandered their gifts of leadership. Their greatest strengths became their greatest weaknesses. They failed miserably in the area of stewardship.

These men are extreme examples of gifting going awry. But none of us are immune to this tendency to squander and misuse our gifts. God has gifted you; how are you stewarding this gift? If you have been given financial strength, good looks, a Shakespearean voice, an attractive personality, or the ability to get people to do what you'd like them to do, how are you stewarding that? The sifting process is guaranteed to affect your giftedness. Are you a great musician? That might be an area of weakness for you. Are you a great communicator? Unless your speaking is submitted to God, you may have a tendency to use your gift for personal gain and selfish ambition. If you are filled with zeal and passion, be careful. Though our Enemy is defeated, he's not stupid. He has had thousands of years to study the human heart, and he knows exactly where we are vulnerable. Often, that point of vulnerability will be very near to your God-given strength.

A while back I was in Dallas speaking for a large group. I was feeling energized, and the audience was electric. I spoke for one hour, and everything seemed to click. When I ended, the audience gave me a standing ovation that lasted for several minutes. When the crescendo abated, I turned to my host and said in a hushed voice, "Something's wrong."

"What in the world could be wrong?" he replied.

"I'm starting to like this too much," I said.

I knew that if I didn't submit this to God, it would be the end of me.

Sharp leaders are clever enough to succeed without God's help. We see it all the time. Secular billionaires, hedonistic celebrities, powerful communicators, and arrogant athletes make the headlines every day. Success in the world's eyes can be gained without acknowledging God, and the same is true in the religious world as well. One television minister who raised funds for victims of the 2008 Sichaun, China, earthquake that left nearly sixty-eight thousand dead remarked in an offhand conversation, "You know, I made two million dollars off that event."

"How do you figure that?" asked a bystander.

"I told the viewing audience that we needed to send one million dollars in aid to the people," he said. "But three million came in. So I did what I said I would do. I sent one million to China to help the victims and kept the other two million."

Wrong. Wrong. Wrong.

The ability to persuade, influence, and speak with conviction can be a powerful tool for success, but unless it is stewarded with humility, integrity, honesty, and obedience, it becomes a tool for serving a leader's selfish desires.

THE RUDDER OR THE ROCKS

The truth is that Satan watches our lives for the areas in which we are most vulnerable. He looks for opportune moments to sink his hooks into our skin. But once we understand his tactics, we can identify the exposed areas of our characters that are prone to attack.

There are two verbs that we need to clarify in our minds and understand in our hearts. One verb relates to temptation and the other to testing. The Enemy of our souls will tempt us. The Greek

GOD IS EVERYTHING
Francis Chan

Shortly after the book *Crazy Love* became popular, I was scheduled to be the keynote speaker at a national pastors' conference. Throughout the morning as I went from room to room I kept hearing my name being whispered over and over again — "Francis Chan. Francis Chan. Francis Chan." There was even a magazine being circulated at the event with my face on the cover. It was disgusting. Who was I to warrant this type of attention?

Right before I was supposed to speak, we were all gathered for a time of worship, and I was struck anew by my own inadequacy in relation to God's greatness. Here I was, hoping to lead pastors into a closer relationship with God, and all I kept hearing about was me. I couldn't stand the dichotomy. Right then and there I broke down and began to weep.

I thought about how everything happening at the conference was exactly what I had never wanted to happen. In that honest moment, I noticed how secretly pleased I was that people were acknowledging me. I remembered how I used to hate it when people gave me glory. But I was also aware of the junk in my own heart — everyone is prone to wander — and I recognized in a fresh way that it was only by the grace and mercy of God that I was even in ministry.

Soon, I was wailing before the Lord. Fortunately, the worship band was still playing loudly — I mean, really cranking it. But then the mood changed, and the worship leader began to play the song "Holy, Holy, Holy." That's when it hit me. I knew there was no way I could speak as planned. Here we all were in this auditorium together worshiping this infinitely vast and holy God, yet my name was being exalted. Something needed to change.

The time of worship ended, and I heard my name being called to the stage. I was just a mess, still crying, snot coming out of my nose. Up I stood. I went to the microphone and started talking about how if all anyone took away from the moment was how great a speaker Francis Chan was, then I had failed. Really, really failed.

My goal all along was to lead people closer to Christ. That's all I had ever truly wanted to happen. I urged people to marvel at the greatness of God. We were serving the God of the universe.

God is everything. I mean everything. We can never forget that fact.

word for "tempt" is *peirazo*, which refers to putting pressure on an object to reach its breaking point. Satan will present you with sinful, idolatrous temptations that are intended to lead you away from the path of righteous obedience to God.

God, on the other hand, will never tempt you, but he will test you. "Testing" comes from the word *dokimazo*, which refers to the act of applying pressure to ratify or certify something. Consider a carpenter who, after building a bookcase, presses on it to check its sturdiness. He purposely applies pressure on his work to test its solidity and reliability. When God tests us, it can feel a bit like that. God applies pressure to our lives because he wants to certify our characters, testing how we respond.

Temptation is intended to lead you to failure and disobedience, while testing reveals the strength of your faith and your convictions. When testing breaks us, leading to failure, this can be a blessing. Godly testing reveals areas of self-sufficiency, dependence on our own gifts and abilities, and lack of faith in God, leading us back to Jesus as the only source of our life and strength.

Take a moment to answer the following questions:

What are your greatest natural-born strengths?

_____

_____

_____

_____

● How well are you stewarding these gifts? How deeply are they submitted to God for his use?

_____

_____

_____

_____

Not only will your gifts and abilities be sifted, but so will your love for God—the quality of your love, that is. I spent eleven years in the rural town of Hilo, Hawaii. The people of this sleepy town were precious and genuine, but among them were many struggling families and broken marriages. In one instance, an attractive young wife showed up at my office asking for advice. She didn't have an appointment but seemed to have an immediate need of attention, so I asked her to sit down and tell me what she was struggling with. She spilled her heart and told me the story of her broken marriage. Her husband had a drinking problem and beat her when drunk. I was flabbergasted that any man would treat a woman this way, and after an hour of listening to her story, my heart went out to her. She needed protection and assistance.

Just as I was feeling a compassion and deep love for this dear lady with such a tragic plight, I heard the Lord whisper, "Be careful. You are loving her with your love. It's corruptible. Instead, love her with my love. It is incorruptible." And it was true. It's easy to grow emotionally connected with people who need help, especially when counseling those of the opposite gender. You feel compassion for them, which can be good, but it can also blind you to the potential for danger. Your heart genuinely goes out to them. You understand their deep needs and want to bring comfort to them. Then gradually you begin to see that you are needed, valued, and respected by the one you are counseling. That's a recipe for disaster. I have seen situations in counseling where well-meaning women will sometimes transfer the affections that belong to their husbands onto a Christian leader they respect and value, particularly when the leader exhibits understanding or compassion toward them. It's not because anyone involved is evil or lascivious. It is simply because we are human beings, prone to temptation.

In my current church building, a rectangular window is built into each of our doors so that no pastor or leader has complete privacy while in his office. Anyone passing by can peek in, and that is intentional. It's not that I don't trust my staff; it's that I don't trust the Devil and I don't want to underestimate our capacity for sin. All of us are susceptible to temptation, and we are foolish enough to trust in our strength.

The fact that we are weak human beings is never an excuse for sin. Our fallen nature explains our weakness in the face of temptation, but it does not excuse it. In Genesis 4:6–7, God has a conversation with Cain about this. Cain's sinful jealousy of his brother, if left unchecked, would consume and control Cain's entire life. So God intervened and warned him: "Then the LORD said to Cain, 'Why are you angry? And why has your countenance fallen? If you do well, will not your countenance be lifted up? And if you do not do well, sin is crouching at the door; and its desire is for you, but you must master it.'"

The truth is that sin crouches at our door as well, and like Cain, we must endeavor to overcome it at every turn. Apart from the grace of God, we will inevitably fail. But as we trust in God's mercy and embrace the good news of the gospel, we find the power to overcome sin. What matters is the tilt of our hearts. Have we grown comfortable with our sin, perhaps excusing our choices and activities because we are, after all, only human? Or do we recognize the power of sin in our hearts and rely on God to fight against it? It's the tilt of our hearts that keeps us afloat and helps us find our way back if we drift.

There's an old saying: "You will be guided either by the rudder or by the rocks." The wisdom of the Scriptures can be a rudder that guides us, reminding us that we should always be cautious when estimating our ability to resist temptation. We should learn to anticipate God's testing and be ready to prove ourselves faithful by making wise choices in the midst of the sifting process. Safeguarding your character and integrity is up to you. Make sure you do this with all diligence. The alternative is the rocks that shipwreck our lives when we overestimate our strength and fall prey to temptation.

Let's pause and do some additional work here. Take some time to think through and answer the following questions:

◣ The greatest temptation I regularly face is:

_____

_____

_____

_____

◣ In order to faithfully resist this temptation, I must rear-range these areas of my life:

_____

_____

_____

_____

STEWARDING YOUR AUTHORITY

Question: What's worse than always being in want? What could possibly be worse than never having enough? Answer: Having everything you've ever wanted without the maturity to sustain it. A wise man once said to me, "There are two pains in life. One is when I don't get what I crave for, and the other is when I get it." The greatest test in my life has not been poverty; it has been prosperity. Having more than you need brings with it a unique set of challenges and temptations. Not everyone can survive success, but by God's grace you can prepare for it while learning to faithfully serve in the trenches and daily humdrum of ministry. The pace of everyday faithfulness is what builds the tensile strength of our humility and dependence on God. Consistently serving God and living in daily obedience prepares leaders to receive accolades and applause with the right attitude, teaching them how to transfer the praise they receive to the one to whom it belongs.

It's not hard to lean on God when times are tough and money is scarce. But when everything is going well, when success is the norm, when we are respected, when people buy our meals and give us the best seat in the house, that's when we are tempted to believe our own positive press. That's when we can grow careless or arrogant or disrespectful. That's when we believe that we are bulletproof and invincible. Paul warns us of this in 1 Corinthians 10:12: "Therefore let him who thinks he stands take heed that he does not fall."

Slim times build stamina, but successes are what God uses to build authority. Authority-building successes may not be the ones the world values in terms of business affluence or financial aptitude. Rather, they may be simple victories like making wise decisions and living consistently in a way that is refreshingly unsurprising. Just as the Greek hero Odysseus resisted the call of the Sirens by binding himself to the mast of his ship, successful leaders often win by staying steady and predictable amidst the enticements that Satan uses to lure gifted leaders to sell their birthrights in moments of anger, jealousy, or lust.

Success comes from living the lifestyle detailed in 1 Timothy 3. Paul encourages people to desire a biblical authority and a holy influence. "It is a trustworthy statement: if any man aspires to the office of overseer, it is a fine work he desires to do" (1 Tim. 3:1). Authority and influence can become intoxicating and addicting if misused, but they are not things a leader should avoid out of fear. Without them, your leadership is simply a suggestion. But in trustworthy, godly hands, authority can redeem a community, influence can convert a bad situation into a beneficial experience, and together these two qualities can build a great movement.

To really grasp what is needed to faithfully steward authority and influence, we need to make this personal. In 1 Timothy 3, Paul lists fifteen character qualities that leaders must model in order to qualify for the responsibility of bearing godly authority. I encourage you to go through the list below and check yourself on a scale of 1 to 10 (1 meaning you need the most help in an area; 10 meaning you typically succeed in this area). Observe the areas where you are most vulnerable. These are the areas where you will probably be sifted soon and where you need to be wary.

◣ **Above reproach.** This trait describes a person with one glaring character deficiency that others can point to, one obvious failing that has never been resolved, one blot on the leader's life that others readily recognize. A character deficiency could be anger that flares up unexpectedly, an immoral tendency, a propensity to lie or be prideful, or a habit of blaming others. Is there one flat spot that others characterize you by?

| 1 | 2 | 3 | 4 | 5 | 6 | 7 | 8 | 9 | 10 |

◣ **Husband of one wife.** This phrase does not simply refer to a leader who has been married only once. For a husband, it describes more literally a "one-woman man." It is one who is faithful to his spouse in body, spirit, mind, emotion, action, and thought-life. Second Peter 2:14 negatively describes a person lacking this character trait as a man "having eyes full of adultery."

| 1 | 2 | 3 | 4 | 5 | 6 | 7 | 8 | 9 | 10 |

◣ **Temperate.** This characteristic describes a person who is self controlled, who lives in moderation. It is someone who refuses to be overly obsessed with any pastime or hobby. It defines a leader who can forego an activity, a cause, or even an occupational mandate for something of greater worth or eternal significance.

| 1 | 2 | 3 | 4 | 5 | 6 | 7 | 8 | 9 | 10 |

◣ **Prudent.** Being prudent means having foresight. It is someone who carries on his present activities and daily conversations while keeping an eye on how these things may affect the larger picture. He is able to bridle temporary appetites in exchange for long-term benefits.

| 1 | 2 | 3 | 4 | 5 | 6 | 7 | 8 | 9 | 10 |

● **Respectable.** A leader who is respectable is one who is regarded by others with esteem and appreciation, whose words influence and whose decisions are trusted.

1   2   3   4   5   6   7   8   9   10

● **Hospitable.** Being hospitable means being friendly and welcoming strangers into your church, social circle, house, and life. This person is willing to help others even when there is no foreseen possibility of reciprocation.

1   2   3   4   5   6   7   8   9   10

● **Able to teach.** A leader must be able to communicate and explain truths in such a way that others comprehend these truths. Teaching can happen verbally, in writing, or by example. Not every leader needs to be a fabulously gifted preacher, Bible expositor, or orator, but every leader must be able to teach truths.

1   2   3   4   5   6   7   8   9   10

● **Not addicted to wine.** This is not a statement of prohibition but of temperance. A leader must be moderate in his food and drink consumption. Truly, a leader cannot be enslaved (addicted) to any substance, be it alcohol, pain medication, pornography, or jelly donuts.

1   2   3   4   5   6   7   8   9   10

● **Not pugnacious.** To be pugnacious means to be belligerent, confrontational, or argumentative. A leader must not be given to anger or venomous reaction when resisted or challenged. He must remain reasonable and unbiased, able to set boundaries, able to acknowledge anger appropriately while not sinning in his anger (Eph. 4:26).

1   2   3   4   5   6   7   8   9   10

● **Gentle.** To be gentle means to have empathy. This character trait understands where another person is coming from. The word in Greek literally means "one who is in or around the likeness of another." It is descriptive of someone who doesn't come to a conclusion until he gathers ample context of another's situation and condition, understanding first why the person is the way he is.

1   2   3   4   5   6   7   8   9   10

◆ **Peaceable.** This characteristic defines a person whose ultimate goal is unity and peace, not dominance. A peaceable person does not give in to every other person's whim. He does not keep the peace at the price of compromise. Rather, a peaceable person seeks solutions and cooperation. He understands that battles and war, while sometimes necessary, come at great cost to all involved. He always pursues peace as a first course of action.

1   2   3   4   5   6   7   8   9   10

◆ **Free from the love of money.** This person stewards well and is faithful with what he presently has. The love of money can put a leader into unnecessary debt. Covetousness is the breeding ground for this dangerous character flaw. Practicing generous giving is the antidote.

1   2   3   4   5   6   7   8   9   10

◆ **Good manager of his own household.** This is a person who prioritizes his own family and whose goal is raising godly children, rather than raising a budget, weekend crowd, or the awareness in others that he is a great leader. It is one whose children have a sense of civility, humility, and respect for others.

1   2   3   4   5   6   7   8   9   10

◆ **Not a new convert.** Immaturity in Christ is not limited to those who have not spent time in church. Rather, immaturity in Christ is measured by a lack of time spent with Christ. Sometimes those who have spent a great deal of time in church have spent very little time with Christ.

1   2   3   4   5   6   7   8   9   10

◆ **Good reputation with those outside the church.** This charac-
terizes a person who is a friend to publicans and sinners and yet
who does not compromise his faith in order to gain their respect.
The respect emerges from the way he lives his faith. This way of
living incurs esteem, even from those outside the church.

1	2	3	4	5	6	7	8	9	10

How did you rate yourself? Are there areas of concern that you
were able to identify? The value in doing this is to discover the low-
lying planks in your life that may be holding back God's authority
from fully resting on you and your ministry. Watch for the red flags.
These may be areas of your life where God is preparing to sift you.
Pray about them and plead for grace that your faith may not fail
when you are sifted and that the result will be growth in character
and godliness so that you are more effective in ministering God's
grace to others.

In addition to the fifteen characteristics of a godly leader that
Paul describes in 1 Timothy 3, there are three heart qualities that a
leader must cultivate: a heart of integrity, a heart of purity, and the
heart of a reformer.

1. A HEART OF INTEGRITY

Leaders must learn to model integrity. In a ministry context, one
opportunity to express integrity that we commonly face is in how we
speak about others. Having integrity means protecting the reputation of those not present in order to gain the trust of those who are.
When I disagree with someone who is not present, it's tempting to
speak bluntly and sometimes inappropriately. We are but a breath
away from gossiping and tearing down others.

But a man of integrity says, "Hold on! It is not my job to ruin
that person's reputation. It's not right for me to criticize him until I
fully understand his side of the story." The Bible warns us not to rush
to judgment, saying, "He who gives an answer before he [fully under-
stands], it is folly and shame to him" (Prov. 18:13). If you are upset
about an incident, do some research first, and allow the other person

to share his or her side of the story. For me to come to a conclusion about another's reputation, heart, spirit, motives, or actions without fully investigating all of the facts would be wrong. Doing so would reveal a lack of integrity. I honor other people by finding out the facts first, and I honor God by trusting him in this process, knowing that he will ultimately expose and judge the truth of the matter.

When you have integrity, those in your presence will say, "You're right. I want to be like that, too!" If I slaughter someone's reputation when he's not there to defend himself, then those listening think, "Whoa! If he slanders that guy when he's not around, then what does he say about me?" Protecting the reputation of those who aren't present gains the trust of those who are. Our integrity will be tested throughout our lives, guaranteed. So prepare yourself by knowing how to respond: by refraining from snap judgments or unfounded gossip.

2. A HEART OF PURITY

In addition to practicing integrity, our hearts need to be constantly run through a purifying filter. Too often, they get clogged with sinful excesses, and the resulting build-up taints our motives. We can grow bitter, cynical, and dark, even prone to unhealthy patterns of sin. Jesus knows the human heart better than anyone else. In Mark 7:21–22 he reminds us to be wise, aware that the heart, apart from the cleansing power God provides for us, is a breeding ground for evil and idolatry: "For from within, out of the heart of men, proceed the evil thoughts, fornications, thefts, murders, adulteries, deeds of coveting and wickedness, as well as deceit, sensuality, envy, slander, pride and foolishness."

I love to be around people whose hearts have been cleansed by Christ, people for whom *repentance* isn't a bad word and confession comes easily. Hudson Taylor, who was a missionary to China in the late 1800s, used to greet his friends by asking, "Have you repented yet today?" He understood that a repenting man is a healthy man, and a repenting church is a healthy church. I want to be like that as well, someone who is eager to repent, rejecting what is evil and loving what is good.

Typically, though, when a situation upsets me, my reaction is nega-tive, the result of something impure residing deep in my heart. It's usually a personal issue that I haven't resolved and have kept buried for years. Something triggers it, and it flares up, irritating me and clouding my judgment. This is what happened to Judas. He criticized Jesus for accepting a costly gift and went on to defend his own self-righteous-ness: "For this perfume might have been sold for a high price and the money given to the poor" (Matt. 26:9). Note that Judas didn't criti-cize Jesus because he was actually concerned about the poor. He did it because he was a thief, pilfering money from the very moneybox he was responsible for keeping. What Judas was really saying was: "Let's sell the perfume and give me the money. I'll hold it under the illusion of giving it to the poor and then help myself to my normal commission." His greed caused his indignation to flare up, and his impure, sinful desires put him on a direct collision course with his Master and Lord.

My own "Judas moment" happened years ago while attending a retirement party for another pastor. He had been in ministry for forty years, and an offering was collected from all the pastors and churches in our district to honor him. It was presented to him as a gift, and at the party they announced the grand total: "We're happy to bless our dear retiring brother with this gift of $40,000!" Everyone applauded. I was clapping too, but on the inside I was disturbed, wrestling with my heart. Forty thousand dollars? This guy already has a house and car, so why does he need $40,000? Do you know how much ministry I could do with that money? I don't even earn that much in a year! In fact, I won't earn that after working for the next three years! This is so unspiritual! After the applause died down, I sensed the Lord quietly addressing me: "Hey, Iscariot!" I immediately realized what the Lord was saying to me. My greed had surfaced—that's why I was indignant. I wasn't motivated by a righteous, godly desire for something good; I was irritated that the money hadn't gone to me.

I find that when I'm indignant about an event or action, it's often because something unhealthy inside of me is surfacing. Instead of acknowledging the root cause, I react by blaming the other person and launching attacks of self-righteousness to defend myself. All the while, I completely miss the real source of the problem: me!

This is one of the ways in which sifting can be very helpful. God uses difficulties in our lives to uncover and reveal any personal issues we haven't dealt with yet. Sometimes these issues may have been hidden for years. We've refused to resolve them, and God brings a trial or a challenge into our life, saying to us, "Now it's time. If we don't deal with this now, you'll continue to hit a ceiling in your growth as my child." It's far too easy to be indignant with others when really the problem is right within our own souls. Thankfully, God's love doesn't allow us to remain trapped in our own self-righteous sin. He lovingly challenges us and confronts us in order to change us.

3. THE HEART OF A REFORMER

The third quality of the heart is just as challenging as the first two and just as vital: we must develop the heart of a reformer. There is a major difference between a reformer and a rebel. Though they may appear similar at first, they are at opposite poles. Both types of leader recognize poor leadership and voice discontent with scriptural violations. But the outcomes are not the same.

A rebel is someone who sees a problem and uses it as justification for slandering and sabotaging. A reformer, on the other hand, sees a problem and uses it as a tool for growth and spiritual advancement. A rebel is a problem finder; a reformer is a problem solver. A rebel is not satisfied even when a problem is resolved; a reformer rejoices when there is resolution. The rebel's heart is fixated on the problem, whereas the reformer's heart is focused on the solution and hurries toward God's best for everyone involved.

Being a rebel is an automatic default for each of us. It's easy to criticize others, pointing out their flaws and failures. Becoming a reformer, though, requires discipline and character. Knowing the difference is crucial in ministry, but choosing to be a reformer over a rebel doesn't guarantee that you'll win the popularity contest or the Miss Congeniality award.

Daniel was one of the Hebrew children deported to Babylon in 597 BC. He was accompanied by Shadrach, Meshach, and Abednego. Though we lose track of the other three after the third chapter of Daniel, we can trace Daniel's life through the remainder of the book. God used Daniel to influence several kings, and his legacy was profound. The Bible tells us that God gave Daniel a spiritual gift of interpreting dreams, as well as something else: "An extraordinary spirit, knowledge and insight, interpretation of dreams, explanation of enigmas and solving of difficult problems were found in this Daniel" (Dan. 5:12). In addition to interpreting dreams, God used Daniel to solve problems, and that set him apart. Though other leaders were interested in promoting themselves at the expense of others, Daniel had the heart of a reformer, working to fix the system so that it would bless and benefit the people of Babylon.

THE LIGHTNING ROD

One piece of advice that I have found very helpful in developing godly character in my life is to find a lightning rod. What does a lightning rod have to do with growing in godliness and stewarding authority? In the Midwest, electrical storms are common, and lightning strikes often. Because it strikes the tallest point in an area, typically you'll see a rod protruding from the roofs of taller buildings. This rod is grounded so that when lightning hits, it conducts the thousands of volts of electricity into the ground, neutralizing the strike. Without a grounded lightning rod, the massive jolt of electricity would spike all the electronic equipment in the building and fry the delicate inner workings of computer circuit boards and more.

We need people in our lives who can serve as living lightning rods. When I'm upset and I want to verbally strike out and attack someone, I turn to my lightning rod, laying out the issues as I see them. My lightning rod listens to me and grounds any destructive current. He helps to neutralize my sinful anger so I don't fry people. Lightning rods listen, and they understand. They allow you to vent, then they accompany you on the journey back to Jesus. They may recognize some validity to your perspective, but they won't let you fry people with any excess emotional baggage you might have. Lightning rods are not "yes" people. They don't have a deep need to be accepted by you. If they have that need, they will end up shouldering your offenses rather than helping you to resolve them.

Lightning rods will become lifelong friends. They will warn you of impending harm and help you avoid the slow overgrowth of self-righteousness. They will help you become the person you've always wanted to be and save you from your sinful patterns and habits by reminding you of God's grace. They will help you truly assess your character and make adjustments.

When you are looking for a person to serve as your lightning rod, my rule of thumb is that brothers help brothers, and sisters help sisters. Setting this healthy boundary will prevent any crossing of wires before things get too far out of hand. Help yourself stay out of trouble: set clear boundaries ahead of time. A second consideration is to know what kind of person you want to become. Your lightning rod can help you become this person by speaking truth and wisdom into your life as well as modeling these traits to you. Do you want to be wise? Slow to anger? Known for your understanding? Then those are the kinds of people you want to befriend. Have you given someone permission to speak into your life to bring correction? It doesn't matter how long you have been in ministry leadership, you will always need someone with permission to speak the truth into your life. We are often blind to our flaws and don't see them unless another person points them out to us. Paul reminds us in Romans 15:14: "I myself also am convinced that you yourselves are full of goodness, filled with all knowledge and able also to admonish one another." Being able to admonish others means being in the business of helping others to see and correct their own faults.

I wish Judas had a lightning rod.

It could have saved him thirty pieces of silver.

YOU ARE THE COMPANY YOU KEEP

A while ago I went to Denver to watch the Colorado Rockies play the Dodgers at Coors Stadium. I knew one of the pitchers for the Dodgers. He grew up in Hilo, and he and his family were members of our church. I sat down smack dab in the middle of about twenty thousand Rockies fans in Coors Stadium. I was engulfed in a sea of purple, the Rockies' team color. It seemed like the whole stadium was cheering for the "wrong" team, as my humble Dodgers were obviously outnumbered. Whenever the Rockies got a good hit, it sounded like the entire state was roaring its approval. Amidst the deafening fans, I would attempt a pitiful little yell, "No!" but you don't want to yell that too loudly unless you are egging for a fight with twenty thousand fanatics. This David versus Goliath competition continued for the first few innings as I sat in a sea of purple.

But then a funny thing happened. After a while I started talking with these enthusiastic Rockies fans, and I started to catch their excitement. When the Rockies had a good hit, they all stood up and yelled, "Yay! Good hit!" And I nodded, "Yeah, I have to admit. That *was* a good hit." A double play followed, and although it was two outs for my Dodgers, I had to confess that it was a great play for any team to make.

In the fourth inning their contagious enthusiasm overtook me. I couldn't help myself. The other team was playing well, and it was only right to recognize that. I can't remember the exact moment, but somewhere between the curve balls and the purple popcorn, I completely switched teams. When the Rockies won, I swelled with purple pride—for the moment, anyway.

So much for my pitcher friend.

This baseball story is a light-hearted illustration of a very serious truth. Proverbs 13:20 says, "He who walks with wise men will be wise, but the companion of fools will suffer harm." Choose wisely who you allow to influence your life, because you will become the company you keep.

Who's standing next to you? With which individuals do you invest the most of your time? Is it a random set of relationships that is based around a common affinity? Is it an arbitrary cadre of acquaintances that share a common like for college football or fishing? You are the company you keep, so choose them well. We are easily influenced.

REMEMBER
Unguarded strengths can become your greatest weakness.

11

Upping Your Skills

Imagine for a moment that I'm an ice skating coach who trains hockey players to be the best they can be. So I gather a group of young men, all eager athletes, all enthusiastic to make it to the big time, all hoping to someday play in the National Hockey League, and I host a big ice skating conference. I bring in the greatest players of all time—Gordie Howe, Guy Lafleur, Wayne Gretzky—as well as current Olympians like Ryan Suter, Paul Martin, and Tim Gleason, and we hold a skating clinic. The pros perform their skills under the lights. They spray ice and demonstrate puck handling skills and show the best moves to make during a power play.

At the end of the conference, I say to my group of young players, "Okay, that's it. On the way out be sure to get a copy of my new book on power skating. While you're at it, pick up a pair of my signature ice skates. Congratulations, you're ready for the NHL."

Do you see any problems with my approach?

Many of the players would probably do exactly what I suggest. They might head home from the conference pumped up about being world-class hockey players. And some of them might even have genuine, raw talent. But some might buy my books and pick up a pair of my skates and then head back to the practice rink, try a few moves, and break their ankles. Some might hang up their skates forever. Others might limp along for a few years wondering why the NHL scouts aren't calling them to play.

These young athletes all want to reach a certain level, but they aren't ready. They haven't been properly trained. Much the same thing can happen when we try to disciple younger leaders. Young leaders want to hit "the big time," however that's defined, but they often leave a conference prepared for nothing but a broken ankle. They have never been trained for the work of ministry.

FAN INTO FLAME

There's a serious misperception that affects church leaders today, and it filters down to the man in the pew as well. The problem is that we believe pastors are born, not made. We can blame it on a faulty understanding of spiritual gifts, perhaps. We read passages like 1 Corinthians 12 and conclude that gifts are simply passed out by God to an eager lineup of hopeful Christians. We assume that we never need to do anything with the gift. It's given to us fully developed, ready to be used; all we need to do is accept it.

Maybe God gives some gifts this way. I do believe in God's calling on people's lives, and I do believe that some people are marked out from an early age, perhaps even from birth, to live lives of effective service for God. I am certainly ready to make allowances for the miraculous, unexpected work of God.

But the normal pattern we observe is that gifts, even spiritual gifts, are manifested in our lives in a rather undeveloped state. They are God's blessing, given to us with the onus on us to grow them and use them wisely. Even Jesus "grew in wisdom and stature, and in favor with God and man" (Luke 2:52 NIV), so wouldn't we need to as well? The apostle Paul reminded Timothy to "fan into flame the gift of God, which is in you through the laying on of my hands. For the Spirit God gave us does not make us timid, but gives us power, love and self-discipline" (2 Tim. 1:6–7 NIV). Notice that Timothy's gift was initially imparted to him supernaturally. It came as a result of Paul's laying on of hands and prayer. But Paul also stressed the need for Timothy to take that gift and turn the spark into a fire: "fan it into flames," Paul said. In other words, do all the work necessary to transform your gift into a mature expression of God's Spirit working through your life.

When we observe others who are successful in ministry, it's natural for us to want that same kind of success, preferably right away, instantaneously. But what we don't see is the years that leader spent honing his craft and developing a particular area of expertise. We don't see the hard work. Think of the long process that it takes to do anything of value. To succeed as a leader, you need to work very hard. This undoubtedly requires a time of preparation, one that continues even after you reach maturity in ministry.

With this in mind, let's consider a few specific case studies:

* A pastor believes he's been given the gift of preaching, yet he finds it takes genuine work to become a dynamic speaker. He may indeed have the gift, but he needs to practice speaking, prepare his messages thoroughly, attend speaking conferences, read books on speaking, and listen to other skillful speakers so he can learn various styles of speaking. Above all, he must practice, practice, practice.

* A Christian leader believes she's been given the gift of hospitality. She has a genuine knack for inviting guests into her home and making them feel welcome. The task feels easy to her. She gains energy from it rather than being drained. But she finds she can still learn and grow in this area. She studies what it means to be hospitable. She takes cooking classes and reads books about decor, conversation, and creating welcoming environments.

* A church planter believes he's been told by God to plant a church and believes that when God calls, God enables. Therefore, he concludes, God will bring this church to reality. Still, while trusting God to do his work, the church planter finds he needs to attend college and seminary to be able to correctly handle Scripture. He attends numerous seminars and conferences and learns to craft vision, gather and inspire a launch team, canvass a neighborhood in search of a viable church planting location, and do any number of the countless tasks that are part of being an effective church planter.

Gifts are given by God, yes. But gifts need to be fanned into flames. Fully developing a gift takes work, a lot of hard work, to be honest.

LEARNING YOUR CRAFT
Larry Osborne

If you are in a season of sifting right now, it may be that God is holding you back so that you can more fully develop the gifts he has given you. God wants to do something mighty through you eventually, but first he wants you to truly learn your craft. He wants to do something within you first so that your gifts burn with intensity and brightness and can never be quenched.

WAX ON, WAX OFF

Let's take another look at those hockey players and give that illustration a twist. I'm still an ice skating coach with a group of young men around me, all eager athletes hoping to make it to the big time and play in the National Hockey League. But now, I try a different approach to training the men.

I say to them, "I want all of you to be great hockey players. The best of the best. If that's what you want too, then meet me here at my ice skating rink tomorrow morning at 5:00 a.m."

The day dawns, the group gathers, and we embark on a curious set of exercises. At first, we don't even hit the skating rink. We go for a five-mile run. After that we lift weights. After that we do a series of exercises designed to strengthen an athlete's core. Then we work on puck handling, defensive moves, and offensive moves. We study tapes of Olympic hockey games. We read books and articles about great skaters. We hit the ice and practice and practice and practice. Days go by. Weeks go by. Even years go by. We keep at our level of intense training, and finally, finally, we produce some exceptionally talented hockey players, some of whom are ready for the NHL.

Do you notice a difference in my training techniques?

- ♦ The first illustration is about nothing but inspiration, giving people the false hope that they can become an overnight success.

◆ The second illustration is more realistic, involving the necessary training time, day in and day out, that is required to achieve a high level of performance.

The second method of training and preparation is the norm in life. If a young concert pianist wants to be exceptional, he spends years learning scales and practicing. He runs up and down the keyboard in endless repetition. He learns music theory. He studies the masters. And he plays and plays and plays and plays.

If a young novelist wants to become a *New York Times* bestselling author, he begins by reading all the masters, both modern and classic — Hemingway, Steinbeck, Fitzgerald, Faulkner. Perhaps he goes to university and earns an MFA. He undertakes endless writing exercises. He keeps a copy of the classic writing book *The Elements of Style* in his back pocket and studies it every morning for years. He might write two or three complete novels and throw them away, considering them practice novels only. He eventually writes a novel and sends it off to test markets and editors, and he rewrites and rewrites and rewrites. All this preparation leads him to the place where he is able to publish masterpieces.

Practice takes work, and sometimes the reasons why God has us in a season of preparation are not obvious to us at first. During this season of sifting, God will often teach us important skills, skills we could not learn any other way. When we are through the season, we may understand, to some extent, why the sifting was needed. We may recognize the change that's occurred inside of us. But while we are in the midst of that sifting season, the reasons for it can be very cloudy.

Have you ever seen the old movie *The Karate Kid*? Not the recent remake, but the original 1984 version starring Ralph Macchio and Pat Morita. The premise is that the young main character, Daniel, played by Ralph Macchio, wants to become the best martial artist he can be. In fact, he *needs* to become the best, so he can defeat his tormenting nemesis, Johnny, and the gang of Cobra Kai students.

Daniel goes to a wise and skilled martial arts teacher, Mr. Miyagi, and begs to be taught karate. Mr. Miyagi agrees to teach him. He orders Daniel to come to his house early the next morning, but Daniel is surprised to find that instead of beginning karate training, Mr. Miyagi has him perform a series of laborious household chores. Daniel spends his time waxing a long line of old cars, sanding a wooden deck, refinishing and painting a fence, and painting the siding of Mr. Miyagi's house. Each chore is accompanied by breathing exercises and involves a specific type of hand and arm movement.

Daniel fails to see the connection between these hard chores and his training, and he eventually feels frustrated, believing he has been duped into free labor, learning nothing of karate. When he expresses his frustration, Mr. Miyagi reveals that all this time, while Daniel has been working, he has actually been learning karate moves through the chores. In one glorious scene, Mr. Miyagi orders Daniel to show him the various skills, one by one, and Daniel can suddenly perform them. He is amazed to find that all of his work has had a purpose all along. Without realizing it, he has become a skilled martial artist.

I realize that it may seem irreverent to compare God's methods to Mr. Miyagi's, and I certainly don't mean to be irreverent. But I find that God works in our lives in much the same way that Mr. Miyagi worked in Daniel's life. As church leaders, we often fail to understand why we are placed in a season of waxing cars, sanding floors, and painting fences. All the while, we are dreaming of the big time — impacting lives for the sake of Christ. Only later when these skills are called upon in a crisis or a moment of great opportunity do we realize we've developed the necessary abilities for healthy ministry. The seasons of laborious, faithful obedience to God's work have prepared us for the present moment.

The prophet Jeremiah once asked God a similar question about God's methodology in training his people. Challenges arose in Jeremiah's life that he couldn't understand, and in response, God said to Jeremiah, "If you have raced with men on foot and they have worn you out, how can you compete with horses? If you stumble in safe country, how will you manage in the thickets by the Jordan?" (Jer. 12:5 NIV).

In other words, God warns the weary prophet that the call to serve the Lord can be very difficult, bringing a man to his breaking point and stretching his natural abilities. Ministry can be like running a footrace against horses or like pushing your way through dense forest. If you wish to operate at that high level of output one day, you must first go through a season of preparation. You must learn how to do the easier tasks—to race with men on foot and to hike through safe country without stopping every five seconds to catch your breath. That's what long seasons of preparation are for. That's why God brings us through them.

What is God taking you through right now? How might this be a season of preparation for something new? There are no certain answers to these questions, so let's do a bit of work, thinking through this. Take some time to answer the following questions.

◗ I believe God is taking me through:

_____

_____

_____

_____

◗ He wants me to learn:

_____

_____

_____

_____

A helpful verse as you think about this is Proverbs 16:9: "The mind of man plans his way, but the LORD directs his steps." In other words, we can make plans and head in certain directions, but the Lord will ultimately establish our future. If you are in a season of sifting right now, it may be because God wants to develop some stronger or more advanced skills in you. I invite you to give yourself more fully to the process. Learn what needs to be learned. Put in the hours of preparation. Call upon God so that you do not lose heart in the midst of the testing, the trials, and the challenges you face. Let me suggest five disciplines that may help you survive and thrive through the sifting season and develop the skills and character that God wants for you:

1. *Commit to constant learning.* An effective leader develops a regimen to constantly increase his knowledge. A leader needs to be a reader and be well-read in a vast and diverse array of leadership areas. Personally, I find my reading pattern takes me to fields other than church planting and ministry formation. For instance, right now I'm reading a book about training horses, but it's also a helpful book on leadership. I know that might sound strange, but as I'm reading I'm learning that a man must be a skilled and steady leader to train horses, and I'm finding many applications to ministry situations I face.

2. *Study the best.* Do this in whichever discipline you want to learn. I encourage young leaders to look for the top speakers and leaders they want to emulate and study what those leaders do. For instance, if you want to be a skilled public speaker, get copies of the top messages, put them in your car, and listen to them on your way to and from work. You can listen to ten in a week, and you will learn to listen with acuity to how gifted speakers phrase their words, how they articulate and flesh out a concept, and so on.

3. *Always be coachable.* Develop the skill of consistently learning from others, of having a teachable spirit. This principle works no matter what level you reach. I find it helpful to have coaches in virtually every area of life: a writing coach, a personal life coach, a long-range planning coach, an executive ministerial coach, and several more. I have an academic endeavors coach because I'm working in the college world now. I have a coach on donor relations and fundraising. Get a coach for the areas that are most important in your life. When tennis star Serena Williams goes on tour she takes along more than her tennis racket. She takes her coach. She's one of the best in the world, so why would she need a coach? Her coach is one reason she's the best. Serena Williams understands the importance of being coached.

4. *Commit to reflection.* It's not only life experiences that will teach you, it's reflecting on those experiences. If you merely go through an experience and don't reflect on it, you will

remember only what you tried before that didn't work. Experience alone does not teach you. You must be disciplined in reflecting on what God has taught you through those experiences. Take your errors and use them to study how you could have done things differently. Let your future inspire you, but let your past mentor you. In the future lies your potential. In your past lie your experiences.

5. *Take joy in progress.* Fanning your gifting into flame can be a long road, but joy can be found along the way. Joy is found in contribution and not in achievement alone. If you take joy only in achievement, you'll be a driven madman. But if you take joy in what you can contribute, you'll have many celebration opportunities along the way. Measure your value in contribution. Have you contributed to a ministry, to someone's life, to another young leader? Have you inspired them? That is cause for great celebration.

RESIST STUBBORNNESS

It's not easy for church leaders to realize they need help with their ministerial skills. Church leaders, particularly church planters and those starting new ministry initiatives, tend to be self-made renegades, men of action who charge hard to perform each task. I encourage you to resist any urge to be stubborn. Take a good, honest look at your skills. Talk them over with trusted advisors. If changes need to be made, if areas need to be improved, take the necessary steps to up your skills.

A church leader I knew believed he was God's gift to preaching. He planted a conservative-oriented church in a rural area of eastern America, and most of the people who came to his church were farmers and dairymen, blue collar workers and lumberjacks. One of the things this planter prided himself on was deep exposition of Scripture. He believed thoroughness was the key component, and so he often preached for forty-five minutes to an hour, sometimes even an hour and fifteen minutes.

Now, I'm not debating the length of sermons. I believe sometimes God can call a church planter to a type of ministry where longer sermons are valued. Mark Driscoll, the senior pastor of Mars Hill Church in Seattle, regularly preaches for an hour, and his messages are said to reach his congregation well. Driscoll has developed a hard-hitting urban church culture where his sermons are geared primarily to young men, and he has worked hard to develop a receptivity to longer, meatier messages. I applaud him for undertaking this ministry well.

This other church leader, however, had not worked to foster that sort of culture. People in his congregation started to grumble. Really, only part of the problem was the length of sermons. The other part was that he struggled in his teaching. His messages were far from dynamic. They dragged on and on, often covering a multitude of subjects and rabbit trails. Frankly, his messages were hard to listen to.

One day an elder at his church took him aside and encouraged him, at very least, to trim ten to fifteen minutes off each sermon. But the pastor refused. He insisted that he was doing God's will by preaching the way he did. Then, a colleague encouraged him to attend a homiletics conference to up his speaking skills. Again, the pastor refused. The apostle Paul wasn't known for being a dynamic speaker, so why should he be? The colleague went to the conference by himself and brought back CDs of the sessions, hoping his friend would at least listen to them. But, yet again, he refused.

Six months later this church split. About forty people of the hundred or so members he had gathered walked out, and it took years and several staffing changes for that church to recover, stabilize, and begin to move forward again. My encouragement is to not be like that leader. Learn to listen to trusted advisors. Work to develop your skills. And become the best you can be for the glory of God.

REMEMBER
It takes a long time to learn how to teach and even longer to learn how to learn.

12

The Classroom for Great Leadership

Brazilian soccer players train in desperate conditions.
Their fields are bumpy, and the conditions are far from ideal, but this is done intentionally, regardless of how much the young hopefuls complain. It is not a matter of money or available resources. The Brazilians have taken home the World Cup trophy several times, and players like Pelé are legendary. So why the archaic conditions?

In an article on the Brazilian method of training, a successful soccer coach said that if these young players can excel on these uneven fields, they will be exemplary on turf that is level and smooth. And if they can go without water for an afternoon's practice in the hot sun, they will develop into consummate players under the lights. Playing soccer in the stadiums will not be an arduous task but something they will execute with ease. And all because of uneven playing fields and training conditions that are less than ideal.

If you're in a difficult season of ministry right now, take heart. God is the ultimate coach. He knows what he's doing. And that's how I want to end this book: with an exhortation to once again commit yourself fully to his ways. We may not always understand God's ways, but we can have confidence that his ways are purposeful, planned, and good.

One of the ways God sifts us as ministry leaders is by asking us to play on an uneven field. We might serve under a poor supervisor, volunteer our time under a rigid pastor, or play second fiddle to a terrible violinist. If we find ourselves in such a situation, we're in good company. The true test of leadership is not how you fare under favorable conditions; it's how you respond when everything goes wrong.

THE BELIEF WINDOW

Some years ago, I visited Israel and walked past the tomb of David. It was bedecked with flowers and wreaths. People were still paying their respects to the greatest king Israel had ever known, hundreds of years later! But consider the way God chose the rulers of his people. David's predecessor, King Saul, was an insecure leader who spent most of his life defending his territory rather than expanding his influence. King Saul's insecurity finally did him in and led to the death of many others under his influence. So how in the world did Saul ever end up as the king of Israel? Well, the answer is clear: Saul was chosen by God. In 1 Samuel 9:17 (NIV), we read that Samuel the prophet was instructed by God to anoint a king: "When Samuel caught sight of Saul, the LORD said to him, 'This is the man I spoke to you about; he will govern my people.'"

Didn't God know that Saul would be a bad king? Didn't he know that David would be forced to flee as a fugitive from Saul's insanity and jealousy? Didn't God know that Saul's fears would bring death to himself and his son, Jonathan? Yes. God knew what he was doing. When things don't go as we expect, we falsely conclude that things did not go as God planned. We tend to define God's goals so that they match the way we want our life to unfold. We assume that the way we see things should be the way God sees them too. But we forget that we have limited vision. We can see only from a limited perspective. God, on the other hand, sees eternity. He sees the end from the beginning. We must develop this caliber of eyesight as well. With an eternal perspective, the whole world seems clearer to us.

The truth is that even in our bodies, we don't actually see with our eyes. Our eyes are only the lens through which we view objects. What we see is actually sensory input that is processed in our brain. The occipital lobe of the brain not only determines the shape and color of objects for us, but it helps us to define what we are looking at. Our eyes are the lens, the means by which we gather input from the world around us, but understanding what we see is a matter of perspective. It requires interpretation, understanding.

So when you look at the world, what do you see? Does the world appear dangerous? Is it friendly? It is positive or negative? Is this situation beneficial or harmful? What should our disposition be? All of these questions take place within us; they are a matter of perspective, the way we understand and interpret the world. And it is this inner reflection that determines our approach to life. In a season of sifting, we must learn to develop a new vision, a fresh perspective on our circumstances, a vision rooted in God's truth. We must learn to process what we see through a different paradigm, one that is informed by the truth about God that is revealed to us in the gospel.

A story is told of a man who looked out his window at the neighbor lady's wash hanging on the clothesline outside her house. "My," he exclaimed to his wife, "she needs to use some bleach on those whites! They are filthy!" The following day he noticed the same soiled clothes on the line. "She'd better change detergents!" The third day, again, he noticed it. "I would be embarrassed to have my clothes washed by this lady!" But on the fourth day, he was surprised at how clean and bright her washing looked. He said to his wife, "Why, she must have changed detergents finally."

"No," his wife replied. "I just cleaned our windows."

The most important decision you will ever make as a leader is to follow Jesus Christ, but the second is the attitude with which you choose to follow Jesus Christ. This perspective will largely determine how you approach life experiences and will shape your behavior, your response to ministry problems, and the way you deal with life's challenges. In many situations, the only difference between what we'd see as an ordeal and what we'd see as an opportunity is your attitude. Each of us is only a change in perspective away from seeing our circumstances as God's good will for our lives instead of a disappointing, frustrating setback.

In front of every leader is a set of windowpanes through which everything is seen. As a leader proceeds in ministry, those panes of glass can get scratched, etched, covered with graffiti, or discolored by what others do and say to us. Each of us is responsible for cleaning those markings constantly to lessen the possibility of faulty attitudes and perspectives. For instance, a jealous coworker might remark how unprofessional your work appears to be. He writes "lackluster" on your window. That marking, if not resolved, will stay there and discolor your attitude about your ministry and affect your work. Another person may comment on how unruly your children are, and another might mention how much you like to be in charge of everything. If the disapproving comments remain, you will see everything through those lenses and start to believe them. You will sabotage your own efforts and underestimate your own potential.

Those comments are difficult to erase, but God's grace makes it possible for us to renew our vision, changing the way we see the world around us through constant washing with the water of God's Word. The eternal Scriptures alone have the power to renew the image of God's Son in you. Never forget that:

- ◆ The most important thing about you is what God says about you.
- ◆ The most important thing about your marriage is what God says about your marriage.
- ◆ The most important thing about your ministry is what God says about your ministry.

Therefore, it is crucial for you to let God's Word write on your window. Learn God's thoughts on a matter, and write down on your plate glass only what God is saying. Let everything else fall subservient to God's eternal Word.

REFUSING OFFENSES

Take a moment to read the following account. Don't skim it. Take your time to read it.

> When the Sabbath came, He began to teach in the synagogue; and the many listeners were astonished, saying, "Where did this man get these things, and what is this wisdom given to Him, and such miracles as these performed by His hands? Is not this the carpenter, the son of Mary, and brother of James and Joses and Judas and

Simon? Are not His sisters here with us?" *And they took offense at Him.* Jesus said to them, "A prophet is not without honor except in his hometown and among his own relatives and in his own household." And He could do no miracle there except that He laid His hands on a few sick people and healed them. And He wondered at their unbelief.

—*Mark 6:2–6, emphasis added*

One surefire way to flatten out your perspective on life is to hold onto an offense over something another has done. And notice that the environment of offense here is defined as "unbelief." Because of unbelief, Jesus could do no miracle in this town. It doesn't say, "He didn't do any miracles." It says, "He could do no miracle." When we hold onto our offenses, we let go of the miraculous.

There will be ample opportunities for you to take offense in the work of ministry. Perhaps you're seldom shown appreciation for the extra effort you exert in outreach. You are overlooked for a pay raise, or you aren't invited to a luncheon. Your opinion wasn't asked, or you weren't given credit. It's easy to take offense. And Jesus, too, had opportunities for taking offense. He was stalked by demons, slandered by leaders, abandoned by family, and betrayed by friends. Yet he refused to be offended by any of this. He did not harbor bitterness against his enemies. Instead, he forgave them.

So must we.

Feeling affronted by another's immaturity or shouldering a misunderstanding shrouds your perspective and reduces your capacity to receive God's intervening power. An unwillingness to forgive cuts us off from the one who has forgiven our offenses. I don't know about you, but I rely on God's power in my life and ministry every day, and because of that, I can't afford to take offense at what people do or say to me. And neither can you. Leave room for the miraculous, for the life-giving grace of God, by refusing to take offense.

You can't afford the cost of being offended. It's not in your budget.

The safest place to take your offenses is to Jesus Christ. When we bring our wounded hearts to Jesus, he converts our pain into a blessing; he takes a liability and makes it a benefit. An offense, when placed under his blood, is stripped of its devious power. Once you put something under the blood of Christ, don't touch it again. Just leave it there and watch to see what God is about to do.

It may be helpful to stop for a moment and ask ourselves a few questions:

◆ What graffiti has been etched on my belief window? What lies have I accepted about myself, offenses I have taken to heart that I need to overcome?

_____

_____

_____

_____

◆ Describe a time when an offense lingered longer than it should have and recall any decisions that would have been affected by it:

_____

_____

_____

_____

A PARADOXICAL EQUATION

How leaders deal with other people's sins is crucial, but how a leader deals with his own sin is catalytic. Consider Achan, who stole costly garments and bars of gold and silver from Jericho (Joshua 7). Achan's sin was invisible to those around him. The gold was stuffed into his clothing and hidden under his bed. But even though it was hidden, it still had an effect on others. The Lord knew of his transgression, and the sin needed to be dealt with.

Because sin is easy to hide, it often leads to a paradox among leaders: some leaders with overt sin in their lives seem to enjoy a great amount of success, while other leaders with no apparent sin in their lives struggle with barrenness.

If only the connection between sin and success were simple! Why doesn't God arrange it so that those who sin don't succeed? He could make all of this simple, straightforward, and clear for us. But it's never that simple. Sin is a propensity we each have to exercise our flesh. Often, what appears to be a God-honoring lifestyle, free from sinful patterns and habits, is simply the result of a lack of opportunity. Many people don't commit certain types of sins simply because they have not yet had the opportunity to do so. There may be a dangerous tendency that lies latent within us waiting for an opportunity, and God knows that if we are put in a position to do so, we will choose to please ourselves over obeying God.

Sin dwells within our hearts. Jesus explains this in Mark 7:21: "For from within, out of the heart of men, proceed the evil thoughts, fornications, thefts, murders, adulteries, deeds of coveting and wickedness, as well as deceit, sensuality, envy, slander, pride and foolishness. All these evil things proceed from within and defile the man." According to Jesus, sin originates in us, not in anyone or anything outside of us. James warns us of this as well, that it is our own evil desire that tempts us, giving birth to sin (James 1:14 – 15). The Enemy may use circumstances or temptations to appeal to our fleshly desires, but the responsibility for what we choose to do is ours. We may try to absolve ourselves of responsibility by blaming others for our choices, but the Bible is clear: the evil we desire and do lies within us. It is present in our hearts in a latent form, ready to surface when the opportunity arises.

I have counseled several ministry leaders who have been disqualified from leadership by their sinful behavior. I consistently find that the fall into sin does not happen overnight. It's not a sudden experience. The truth is that our Adversary knows the Scriptures better than we do. There is not one demon in the universe who is an atheist. Satan knows that the wages of sin is death, but his greatest desire is *not* that we receive the immediate consequences of our sin. One of Satan's most cunning ploys is delaying the consequences of our sin in order to ensure our eventual and total destruction. When we violate our conscience and dabble in sin, whether it begins with an emotional affair or a compromise in other areas, the Enemy suspends the cost of that spiritual debt. Why? Because he knows the Scriptures. He's read Ecclesiastes 8:11: "Because the sentence against an evil deed is not executed quickly, therefore the hearts of the sons of men among them are given fully to do evil." When we quietly defy God's laws and fail to suffer immediate consequences, we are inclined to dabble again and again. Eventually, over time, we sear our conscience and lose any fear of the Lord or his judgment on our sinful behavior. We are now trapped in our sin, unaware that Satan has ensnared us.

Eventually, what is hidden will be brought into the light. It will be plastered on every marquee. Every news headline will seem to speak of your sin. When this happens, you will know you have been sifted by the Adversary and your faith has failed. You were deceived by silence, the lack of an immediate rebuke from the Lord. In most cases, you will find yourself in danger of losing your marriage, your family, and your ministry. Satan will work you to the edge, and when he has you comfortable with your sin, he will pull the carpet out from under you, hoping everything falls apart.

Here's my warning to you: If you find yourself in a habitual pattern of sin and are not experiencing any consequences, fall on your knees immediately and repent. Cry out to the Lord for his mercy. Let your heart default to running to God. Why? Because you are being set up for a fall. Satan doesn't just want your hand slapped. He wants to destroy you. He plays for keeps. Sin is not a game, a diversion to occupy our free time. It is a deadly enemy that must be dealt with by taking decisive action. As leaders, we must constantly examine our lives to see if habits of sinful behavior are present. In other words, keep short accounts with God. Invite his discipline as evidence of his gracious love for you.

Some leaders mistakenly conclude that there are acceptable, politically correct sins and that there are no consequences when they engage in these vices. Sometimes a leader believes he has matured beyond certain safeguards. Perhaps he is consistently given preferential treatment or begins to rely on his past success and neglects the practice of spiritual discipline. The result is a ministry that appears to have a high impact but is actually characterized by shallowness and a lack of godly character. You may have a popular message, but inside you are still driven by anger, pride, or cynicism. You may be able to fill rooms, perhaps even stadiums with the crowds who want to hear you, yet your ministry is lacking in spiritual maturity, depth, and true righteousness.

There are no acceptable or politically correct sins. A leader is not less prone to fall once he becomes a leader. If anything, he is even more susceptible to falling. As a leader, even greater safeguards need to be undertaken in your life. Even more diligence is necessary. Even more discretion should be exercised. Not dealing with your sin will prove devastating. Throughout the sifting process, God will give you regular invitations to reconnect with the message of the gospel and the power of the Holy Spirit. Your sin will be exposed and confronted, and you will have opportunities to see the old man fall away and the new man rise.

MORE THAN ENOUGH

Several years ago, I checked myself into a no-talking Catholic monastery in the remote hills of California. I had come to a tipping point where an unending litany of expectations and responsibilities had me running at a relentless pace. I was caught in a mode of self-destruction. Many years of ministry at this unremitting pace had trained my system to refuse rest, so I fed myself on one big thing after another, running from one ministry high to the next. For me, the road to success and the road to a nervous breakdown had become the same road.

In this time of solitude, I asked God to quiet every voice except his own. At this rural monastery I learned to differentiate his voice from the others in my heart. On the third day of quiet, God began to drill down deep into me. I could feel the sifting. It began with two fierce questions. The first took me nearly a day to answer honestly. "Would you serve me in obscurity for the rest of your days if I asked?" God's question took me by surprise. Why would he want me to serve in obscurity and evaporate into thin air? After several lame attempts to qualify my answer and justify myself to him, I finally surrendered and consented. "Yes, I will serve you in obscurity if you so desire."

The second of God's questions held no reprieve. "Am I enough?"

You can give pat answers to college professors and classroom buddies, but you can't lie to God. It's best to be brutally honest when he asks you a question. Surely, Jesus is more than enough for me, but that would obviously mean a successful church *plus* Jesus, right? Of course that would be enough for me.

But that's not what God asked.

That day, sitting in the silence of the monastery, I finally understood the truth of what had been driving me to the point of exhaustion. For me, Jesus alone had not been enough. That was the chink in my armor. I had been pursuing Jesus plus the other things I wanted, the things that would really give me satisfaction, the things that would really give me the security, the joy, the identity I truly wanted. God reminded me that Jesus alone was more than enough for me, though inside I sensed that he wasn't. Something in my heart needed to change.

Let me invite you to get on your knees before the Lord right now with that same question. Is Jesus enough for you? Don't give a theologically correct answer. Take time to answer it honestly. Knowing what you want in addition to Jesus is key to defeating the lies of the Enemy. If Jesus isn't enough for you, the Adversary will provide as many substitutes as you could want.

Take a few minutes to ask yourself:

- ♦ Is Jesus enough, even when I don't feel successful?
- ♦ If my staff and leaders don't see the church I lead as successful, is Jesus still enough?
- ♦ Is Jesus enough when I struggle financially?
- ♦ If Jesus asks me to serve in obscurity the rest of my life, will Jesus still be enough?
- ♦ If success never comes the way I once dreamed it would, will Jesus still be enough?
- ♦ When I am not as popular as the guy down the street, is Jesus enough?
- ♦ When I encounter seemingly unending problems in the process of leading a church, is Jesus enough?

As we have seen, some sifting will originate from hell, and some from heaven, but both can prove fruitful by the way we choose to respond. Peter, the first pastor called by Jesus, gives us some wise advice in 1 Peter 4:19 (NIV): "So then, those who suffer according to God's will should commit themselves to their faithful Creator and continue to do good." Peter indicates in this passage that there is a way to suffer that is according to the will of God, and there is a way that we can suffer that is not according to his will. The question is not whether we will suffer. The question is how we choose to suffer. We can suffer poorly, relying on our own resources, taking offense at what others say, growing bitter because we aren't getting what we think we deserve. Or, we can suffer according to God's will, a type of suffering that confirms that God is our first love, our great reward, and experience the deepening of his power and presence within us. We can suffer and struggle in a way that bears fruit, revealing that Jesus is enough for us, that he is all that we need.

The suffering that we experience is never the goal in sifting. It is only a means to a greater end: knowing and walking with Christ. Sifting teaches us to establish a pattern of obedience. It humbles us and breaks us of our self-sufficiency, leading to greater dependence on Jesus. We learn to deal promptly with our sin and find that we are weaker than we ever knew, that we need a Savior, not just good advice.

Sifting leads us to a new level of participation in the mission and ministry of Jesus. Christ invites us to walk with him in partnership, to serve alongside him in ministry through the power of the Holy Spirit. Jesus invites us to a relationship with him, but it is a friendship where we serve together. After Peter was sifted and tried, he met with Jesus again on the shore of the Sea of Galilee. Jesus invited Peter to take up the call to shepherd, to join him in his great mission as a partner in ministry. "Feed my sheep," he said to Peter, inviting him to a new purpose in life.

The truth is that our potential is found in what lies ahead of us, not in what lies behind. Past trophies are empty of potential. Paul knew this, and he refused to put his hope in his past success—or

JESUS IS ENOUGH

Francis Chan

What does that actually mean: "Jesus is enough"?

Remember the story of the transfiguration in Matthew 17? Maybe you've studied this passage before or even preached on it. Let's look at it again.

Jesus led three of his closest disciples, Peter, James, and John, on a hike up the side of a high mountain. It was just the four of them on this journey. The other disciples and crowds of followers were not invited along. When they reached the top, something very strange took place. Instead of lighting a campfire and cooking some food, something they might expect to happen on a hike, Jesus began to glow supernaturally.

Can you imagine how strange that must have been for Peter, James, and John? I can only imagine how crazy it would be if I were on a hike with Larry and Wayne and, all of a sudden, one of their faces started to look like it was on fire! The Scriptures tell us that Jesus' face shone like the sun, and his clothes became as white as the light. And suddenly Moses and Elijah appeared, talking with Jesus.

Peter, for one, could not believe his eyes, but he was ever the practical man. "Hey Jesus," Peter exclaimed. "Let me build three shelters — one for you, one for Moses, and one for Elijah."

While Peter was still speaking, a bright cloud enveloped them all, and a voice from the cloud rumbled forth and said, "This is my Son, whom I love; with him I am well pleased. Listen to him!"

When Peter, James, and John heard this, they fell facedown on the ground, trembling. That was the end of the moment of transfiguration. Jesus walked over to the three disciples on the ground, shook them lightly, and encouraged them not to be afraid. When the three got up, they saw no one on the mountaintop except Jesus.

Put yourself in that scene. Picture the vibrancy of Christ, the grandeur of who he is. That's the one you serve.

That's Jesus.

> And that's what that phrase, "Jesus is enough," is pointing at. No matter how big we get or how small we remain, Jesus is enough. No matter the size of our congregation or how dysfunctional it seems, Jesus is enough. No matter if we never publish articles or speak at national conventions, or no matter if we do, Jesus is enough. No matter if there are days we long to quit or days when we absolutely love what we do, Jesus is enough.
>
> Are we always reminding ourselves of the sufficiency of Jesus? If all else goes away in our lives, we will still have him.
>
> Jesus is who we truly need.

failure. Paul writes in Philippians 3:13–14, "Forgetting what lies behind and reaching forward to what lies ahead, I press on toward the goal for the prize of the upward call of God in Christ Jesus." Your future will largely be determined by how you choose to respond to the seasons of sifting that God brings into your life. Yes, there will be times when the Enemy is sifting you, when you sense your life under attack and you must resist direct temptation, but remember that even in these seasons God is at work.

Jesus proved this in Luke 4. The chapter begins with these words: "Jesus, full of the Holy Spirit, returned from the Jordan and was led around by the Spirit in the wilderness for forty days, being tempted by the devil" (Luke 4:1–2). Even though Jesus was full of the Holy Spirit, he still faced a season of sifting that would lead to a time of ministry, provided he passed the test.

Jesus stood unshakable in his season of sifting and refused to surrender to Satan. Luke 4:14 records the ending of the scene: "And Jesus returned to Galilee in the power of the Spirit, and news about Him spread through all the surrounding district."

Do you see the important difference here? Jesus went from fullness to power. Though he was already full of the Spirit, the sifting process ratified God's calling on his life, releasing him into a new season of authority and ministry.

The same can be true for us.

This is what heaven longs to applaud: authentic servant-leaders whose ministries are ratified by the Spirit of God, whose faith remains steadfast after a season of sifting. These leaders know that the core of their success is not found in learning the newest strategies for increasing volunteerism, hosting a successful building campaign, or marketing their church through web-based innovation. They are saints, upheld by integrity, and marked by God's power. They are the ones heaven has been waiting for.

Perhaps it's time for you to leave the desert.

The harvest is ready. Are you?

REMEMBER

Jesus is always more than enough for us, but we will not know it until our faith has been tested.

Epilogue
Sifted for the Sake of Others

There are different fuels for different purposes. Gasoline is a volatile fuel. Competitive race car drivers sometimes desire something even more combustible, so they add nitric oxide to the mix. Oil is another fuel, though not as explosive; neither is the diesel that burns in tractors.

Some fuels are good and some destructive. They all are flammable and can produce inordinate amounts of energy, but some fuels destroy the insides of the engine, shortening its life with each ignition.

Different mixtures fuel different leaders. Greed is a powerful fuel that can drive a person. Other fuels include insecurity, pride, anger, disgruntlement, competitiveness, or a need for value and affirmation. These are things that can keep leaders up at night and wake them in the mornings. Some are powerful enough that leaders sacrifice everything, including families and relationships, on the idolatrous altar they have created to feed their desire.

Often, when we boil everything down, we find our honest goals are unspoken motivations such as:

- I want to feel good about myself.
- I want to be admired by my peers.
- I want people to like me.
- I just want lots of people to come.
- I want to be highly effective so I will become known as successful and spiritual.

◆ I want to have a church just like Andy Stanley's or Mark Driscoll's (or whichever big name leader you admire).

Many great leaders start off with the wrong fuel mixture. It gets them going, but it won't sustain them in the long run. What starts off as insecurity can be converted, but every ministry leader needs to learn the art of in-flight fuel changes. Often we are not able to check out of the ministry for a few years to make the switch, so we need to change fuels en route. And the greatest fuel? Paul nailed it in 2 Corinthians 5:14 (NIV): "Christ's love compels us."

Paul goes on to explain the love of Christ, the love that compels him, driving him forward in all that he does and says: "He died for everyone so that those who receive his new life will no longer live for themselves. Instead, they will live for Christ, who died and was raised for them" (2 Cor. 5:15 NLT).

Paul reminds us that when we are compelled by the love of Christ, we no longer live for ourselves. We do everything for the sake of Christ, who gave everything to save us and make us his. We are compelled — pushed and driven — by love, love for the lost, love for those whom Christ came to save.

Always remember the vision of Christ, the focus of his love. Luke 19:10 sums it up well: "For the Son of Man has come to seek and to save that which was lost." One of the mottos I live by is that we must connect everything we do to a soul. If the activity or endeavor I'm involved in doesn't bring souls to Christ, I rethink it. It's easy to get involved with benevolent endeavors of justice and mercy, human compassion, and protecting human rights. There's nothing wrong with any of those noble callings. But we cannot engage in these gallant endeavors to the exclusion of what is most eternal: the salvation of the lost. No other group on the face of the earth has been given the exclusive assignment to offer redemption to mankind. It is the exclusive assignment given to the church!

A volunteer was setting up a speaker for our morning service that was set to begin in two hours. He struggled to lift it higher on its stand and then tightened the fastener down, stabilizing it at just the correct height. I walked by, and after thanking him for his service, I asked innocently, "What are you doing?"

"I'm setting up a speaker, pastor."

I replied, "No, you're not."

"Yes, I am. I do this each Sunday morning."

"But you're not," I pressed.

Quizzically, he said, "Then what *am* I doing?"

I said, "You are making it possible for a person who comes to church, maybe for the first time, to hear the gospel preached clearly, without static or feedback. And when I give an invitation at the end of the message, and he raises his hand to receive the Lord, I didn't lead him to Christ. We did so, together."

I walked over to the children's ministry where a young volunteer was changing a baby's diaper. "What are you doing?" I asked.

"Changing a diaper," she said confidently.

"Oh no, you're not," I said.

"Oh yes, I am!" she replied, wrinkling her nose.

Smiling, I repeated, "No, you're not."

She put down the diaper, faced me and said, "Just what *am* I doing, pastor?"

I said, "You are making it possible, maybe for the first time, for a young mother to listen to the gospel without distraction because she's trusted you with her child. And because of that, when God speaks to her heart and she responds to the invitation to receive redemption, I didn't lead her to Christ. We did it, together."

It's critical that we understand this and are prepared to help others understand it as well. In everything we do, no matter how small or inconsequential it may seem, there is an eternal purpose. The style we use to present the gospel is not the main thing. Neither is the method. How well known you are is useless. What matters most is that you are compelled by the love of Christ, that you find the lost and share this love, the truth of God's forgiveness and grace revealed in the gospel of Jesus Christ, with them.

WAITING FOR A RESCUE

I will never forget Bully. Although a gentle man, he got his nickname in years past when he was a gruff construction worker who barked more than he talked. Bully was in our congregation when I was first

THE FUEL THAT DRIVES YOU

Francis Chan

Asking good questions helps to reveal the motives that drive you in ministry. Here are some honest ways to scrub your soul by intentional evaluation. In fact, these are the six questions that I ask myself before every speaking engagement.

1. *Am I more concerned about what people think of my message or about what God thinks about my message?* If I am more concerned about people, then I deliberately picture God in the room. Speak to him. Focus on him. I remind myself that people may or may not like my message, but what I am really after is hearing from above, "Well done, good and faithful servant."

2. *Do I genuinely love the people in this congregation, or am I more focused on the number of people in attendance?* I deliberately look at my congregation and pray that God will give me a genuine love for my people.

3. *Am I presenting this message because I genuinely care for people's spiritual growth and encouragement, or am I speaking what people want to hear rather than what God wants me to say?* It's easy to fall into the trap of preaching messages we know will guarantee the attraction or approval of the crowd.

4. *Am I depending on the Holy Spirit's power or on my own cleverness?* We all have talents, and we know what they are. There's nothing wrong with using great illustrations and anecdotes, but at the end of the day, we must let the Holy Spirit, not our sense of humor, persuasive words, or winsome smile, move our congregation.

5. *Am I applying the teachings of Scripture to my own life?* Paul tells Timothy to watch his own life and doctrine (1 Tim. 4:16). We are also responsible

for ensuring that we are continuously in God's Word and growing spiritually.

6. *Will the event I am leading draw more attention to me or to God?* After I speak, will the people think more about the God described in Matthew 17, his voice and power, or more about how smooth I am as a communicator?

starting out in Hilo. One day, as we were talking, I noticed some scars on his hands, and I asked him, "Bully, how'd you get so many cuts?"

He unfolded the story of a tsunami that hit the Hilo Bay back in the sixties, recounting, "I was working above the bay that our home overlooks. One morning, the tide receded so much that the children ran out to catch fish in the tide pools left behind. We'd never witnessed the tide so low before, and it gave the kids an unprecedented opportunity to play and romp through the reefs that now protruded above the waterline like newly formed islands in the ocean. But what we didn't know was that the ocean was preparing to unleash the largest tsunami our sleepy little town had ever experienced.

"Within minutes, a sixty-foot wave charged our unsuspecting town with a force we'd never seen before. The hungry waters rushed inland. Like bony fingers, the waters scratched and pulled homes, cars, possessions, and people back into a watery grave. The devastating power of that wave left in its wake twisted buildings, shattered windows, splintered homes, and broken dreams. I ran as fast as I could to our home, where I found my wife sobbing uncontrollably. 'Robby is missing,' she shouted. 'I can't find Robby!'

"Robby was our six-month-old child who was asleep in the house when the ocean raged against our helpless village. I was frantic as I looked over the shore strewn with the remains of the frail stick houses that were now piled in heaps along the sands. Realizing that another wave may soon be following, I began running on top of the wooden structures, tearing up pieces of twisted corrugated roofs that were ripped like discarded remains of a demolition project. I tore up one piece after another running over boards and broken beams until I heard the whimpering of a child under one of the mattresses that had gotten lodged beneath an overturned car.

"I reached under and pulled up my little son, Robby. I tucked him under my arm like a football player running for the end zone, then I sprinted back over the debris until I reached my wife. We ran for higher ground, hugging our child and one another, thanking God for his mercy.

"Just then, my wife said, 'Bully, your feet and your hands. You're covered in blood!'

"I had been wearing tennis shoes, and I didn't realize that as I ran over the wreckage, I was stepping on protruding nails and screws that had been exposed in the rubble. And as I pulled back the torn corrugated roofing looking for Robby, the sharp edges tore into my hands."

I stood stunned by the intensity of the event. "Didn't that hurt?" I asked, not knowing what else to say.

"No," he replied. "I was so intent on finding my boy that nothing else mattered."

I couldn't get the image of Bully searching for his son out of my mind for several days after that. Each time I thought of Bully rescuing his son, I couldn't help but think of Jesus and his love for us. His suffering was secondary to finding those who were lost and waiting for a rescue.

You may be experiencing a season of sifting right now. Perhaps you have just been through a sifting experience: a trial, a challenge, a time of testing. You may be struggling with disappointment, wondering why this has happened, wondering what God's purpose is in your suffering and struggle. As we have seen, God uses these times and seasons to refine us and ratchet us back to who he wants us to be. Sifting is God's intentional way of making us more like Jesus, people who are compelled by the love of God and willing to sacrifice everything for the sake of the gospel.

Let me encourage you to run in such a way that you win. May the love of Christ compel you to finish well, and may you bring many home to finish with you.

Acknowledgments

Thank you to Todd Wilson and Exponential Network, Ed Stetzer from LifeWay Research, the forty-three national leaders who participated in the Exponential Survey from which parts of this book were gleaned, Ron Johnson from Accelerate, Ryan Pazdur, Josh Blunt, the whole team at Zondervan, agent Greg Johnson at the WordServe Literary Group, Mark Sweeney at Leadership Network, and editor Marcus Brotherton.

My deepest appreciation goes to my family for attending the journey over these last three-and-a-half decades of ministry. I can identify the seasonal changes over the years, the ministry intersections that marked a new beginning, and the seasons of sifting when I thought all was lost. To see my children walking with Christ and my wife still by my side is reward abundant for whatever small price I was asked to pay.

About the Author

Wayne Cordeiro is senior pastor of New Hope Christian Fellowship in Oahu, Hawaii, which is listed as one of the top twenty-five most influential churches in America and one of the top ten most innovative.

Wayne is a church planter at heart and has been instrumental in planting more than 114 churches. Through New Hope International, the church planting division of the ministry, seventy churches have been established in the Pacific Rim countries of the Philippines, Japan, Australia, and Myanmar, as well as in Hawaii, California, Montana, Washington, and Nevada. At last count, more than one hundred thirty thousand people have made first time decisions for Christ through these churches.

Wayne is now in the process of decentralizing New Hope Christian Fellowship into individual churches, while developing servant leaders for each. His plan is to leave behind twenty-five New Hope churches in the city that will individually grow to transform their communities.

He is an avid builder of emerging leaders. Through mentoring programs, internships, and leadership practicums, Wayne has spent much of his life developing the ministry potential of others.

In addition to his responsibilities at New Hope Oahu, Wayne is chancellor over his alma mater, New Hope Christian College (previously known as Eugene Bible College). NHCC is now part of a consortium of colleges with locations in Hawaii, Myanmar, and Japan.

Wayne has authored eleven books, including *Doing Church as a*

Team, Dream Releasers, Seven Rules of Success, Rising Above, Attitudes That Attract Success, The Divine Mentor, Leading On Empty, and *The Irresistible Church.* Wayne is also the author of the *Life Journal,* which is used by thousands of churches worldwide in bringing people back to the Word of God.

Wayne and his wife, Anna, have been married for more than thirty-eight years. They have three married children and six grandchildren and live in Oregon and Hawaii.

SPECIAL THANKS

Thank you to two of my dear ministry friends, Larry Osborne and Francis Chan. We met for a day in my office discussing what ministry leaders and church planters most struggle with. After a day of visitation, I began writing. It was with their ideas and advice that these thoughts were recorded. Both men also read the manuscript after it was completed and offered feedback.

Larry Osborne has served as a senior and teaching pastor at North Coast Church in Vista, California, since 1980. He has helped oversee the growth of the church from a fledgling group of 128 meeting in a rented school to a multi-site ministry that reaches more than nine thousand in weekend attendance. North Coast Church has been recognized as one of the ten most influential churches in America as well as one of the most innovative.

Larry is also an author and a nationally recognized trainer of pastors. His books include *Sticky Church, Sticky Teams, Ten Dumb Things Smart Christians Believe, Spirituality for the Rest of Us,* and *The Unity Factor: Developing a Healthy Leadership Team.* He travels extensively, speaking at conferences and mentoring pastors and church planters across the country.

In addition to his work as a pastor and writer, Larry also serves as an adjunct professor in the doctoral program at Trinity Evangelical Seminary and as president of the North Coast Training Network, an arm of North Coast Church dedicated to helping pastors across the country maximize their ministry.

Larry holds both a Master of Divinity degree and a doctorate from Talbot Theological Seminary. He and his wife, Nancy, live in Oceanside. They have three grown children.

Francis Chan is the bestselling author of the books *Crazy Love*, *Forgotten God*, and *Erasing Hell* and the host of the *BASIC* DVD series, a series of short films that encourage people to reclaim the church as Scripture describes it to be.

Francis is the founding pastor of Cornerstone Church in Simi Valley, California, and is the founder of Eternity Bible College. He also sits on the board of directors of Children's Hunger Fund and World Impact.

A frequent speaker at conferences around the country, he holds a bachelor's degree from Master's College, and a Master of Divinity from Master's Seminary.

Francis lives in northern California with his wife, Lisa, and their five children.

About the Exponential Series

The interest in church planting has grown significantly in recent years. The need for new churches has never been greater. At the same time, the number of models and approaches is expanding. To address the unique opportunities of churches in this landscape, Exponential Network, in partnership with Leadership Network and Zondervan, launched the Exponential Series in 2010.

Books in this series:

- Tell the reproducing church story.
- Celebrate the diversity of models and approaches God is using to reproduce healthy congregations.
- Highlight the innovative and pioneering practices of healthy reproducing churches.
- Equip, inspire, and challenge kingdom-minded leaders with the tools they need in their journey of becoming reproducing church leaders.

Exponential exists to attract, inspire, and equip kingdom-minded leaders to engage in a movement of high-impact, reproducing churches. We provide a national voice for this movement through the Exponential Conference, the Exponential Initiative, Exponential Venture, and the Exponential Series.

Leadership Network exists to accelerate the impact of 100X leaders. Believing that meaningful conversations and strategic connections can change the world, we seek to help leaders navigate the future by exploring new ideas and finding application for each unique context.

For more information about the Exponential Series, go to *www.exponential.org/exponentialseries*.

About Leadership Network

Since 1984, Leadership Network has fostered church innovation and growth by diligently pursuing its far-reaching mission statement: *To identify high-capacity Christian leaders, to connect them with other leaders, and to help them multiply their impact.*

While specific techniques may vary as the church faces new opportunities and challenges, Leadership Network consistently focuses on bringing together entrepreneurial leaders who are pursuing similar ministry initiatives. The resulting peer-to-peer interaction, dialogue, and collaboration—often across denominational lines—helps these leaders better refine their individual strategies and accelerate their own innovations.

To further enhance this process, Leadership Network develops and distributes highly targeted ministry tools and resources, including books, DVDs and videotapes, special reports, e-publications, and free downloads.

For additional information on the mission or activities of Leadership Network, please contact:

Leadership✳Network

800-765-5323
www.leadnet.org
client.care@leadnet.org

Sticky Teams

Keeping Your Leadership Team and Staff on the Same Page

Larry Osborne

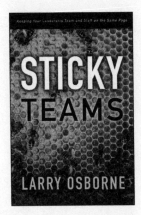

Serving as a church leader can be a tough assignment. Whatever your role, odds are you've known your share of the frustration, conflict, and disillusionment that come with silly turf battles, conflicting vision, and marathon meetings.

No doubt, you've asked yourself, "How did it get this way?"

With practical and accessible wisdom, Larry Osborne explains how it got this way. He exposes the hidden roadblocks, structures, and goofy thinking that sabotage even the best intentioned teams. Then with time-tested and proven strategies, he shows what it takes to get (and keep) a board, staff, and congregation on the same page.

Whatever your situation—from start-up, to midsized, to megachurch—Osborne has been there. As the pastor of North Coast Church, he's walked his board, staff, and congregation through the process. Now with warm encouragement and penetrating insights, he shares his secrets to building and maintaining a healthy and unified ministry team that sticks together for the long haul.

Available in stores and online!